Springs of Hope

The Story of

Johann Sebastian Bach

By

Joyce McPherson

This book is dedicated to Diane, Bill and Jennifer
with fond memories of the childhood we shared.

Table of contents

Timeline

1685	Johann Sebastian Bach is born on March 21st at Eisenach and baptized March 23rd
1692	Enters school at the St. George Latin School in Eisenach.
1694	His mother dies on May 1st.
1695	His father dies on February 20th. Sebastian leaves Eisenach to live with his brother Johann Christoph in Ohrdruf and enters the Lyceum School.
1700	Leaves Ohrdruf for St. Michael's School in Lüneburg.
1703	Court musician at Weimar March-September and is appointed organist in Arnstadt August 9th.
1707	Organist at St. Blaise's Church in Mühlhausen from June 15th, and marries Marie Barbara Bach at Dornheim on October 17th.
1708	Organist and chamber musician to Duke Wilhelm Ernst at Weimar in June.
1717	Capellmeister to Prince Leopold at Cöthen.
1720	Wife, Maria Barbara, dies.
1721	Marries Anna Magdalena Wilcke at Cöthen December 3rd.
1723	Cantor at St. Thomas Church in Leipzig and director of music at St. Thomas School.
1736	Appointed honorary court composer to the Elector of Saxony on November 19th.
1747	Visits court of Frederick the Great at Potsdam May 7-8th.
1750	Dies on July 28th

Chapter One

Papa's Violin

A lilting melody filled the room as the violin bow slid across the strings. Up and down the scale the violin sang. Sebastian watched his father play and felt a golden happiness flow from the music.

His father let the last note fade away, and then reverently placed the instrument in its case. The sun gleamed on its polished surface, and Sebastian gently touched the violin. "Could I learn to play, Papa? I'm almost five years old, and see how big my hands are."

His father took Sebastian's hands in his own, and studied them for a moment. "Let us see what you can do."

Sebastian eagerly picked up the violin and rested it on his shoulder. He had to stretch his arm to put the bow in the right place, but his father guided his hand until he had the correct position. Sebastian pulled the bow across the string,

1

and it made a small squeak.

His older sister Maria Salome peeked around the door. "Come quickly, everyone. Sebastian is learning to play the violin!"

The rest of the family, along with his father's apprentices, hurried into the room. His mother carried her bundle of mending, and his older brother Christoph held a sheaf of sheet music in his inky fingers. He was visiting from his apprenticeship in Erfurt where he studied organ under the great Pachelbel.

His brother Jakob followed, looking critically at Sebastian. "The violin is too big."

Sebastian ignored him and listened instead to the violin. He knew he could make it sing. Another squeak came from the instrument, and Sebastian tried again. A sweet note trilled under his fingers.

His mother smiled. "You will be a musician like your father someday."

For the next few months Sebastian greeted his father everyday when he returned from his afternoon duties and asked for another lesson on the violin. Sometimes his father shook his head. "You are too impatient. You must practice until you have mastered your exercises. Then, I can teach you more."

Sebastian worked on the basic drills his father gave him. It was hard to take these slow steps when every bit of him wanted to race ahead and learn to play real music.

Every day he practiced for his mother in the kitchen while she prepared dinner, and sometimes he played in the evening when the family gathered to make music. These evenings were not as plentiful as Sebastian liked because his father directed the town musicians. They served as house orchestra to Duke Johan Georg and often performed at night.

One day Christoph arrived with exciting news. The church in Ohrdruf had hired him to be their organist. Sebastian admired his tall brother Christoph, whose music poured from the organ in rich melodies. Old Cousin Johann Christoph, who was church organist in Eisenach, invited the young man to play the organ before he left for his new job.

As Sebastian sat in church, the booming music filled him with a solemn feeling. The minister read the scripture, and the organ and choir responded with a hymn. As the family walked the steep cobbled street toward home, Sebastian still heard the music in his head.

"Papa, how can I learn to play music like Christoph?"

"Do you remember the scripture reading today?" his father replied.

Sebastian tried to think, but the music took away his thoughts.

His father laughed. "You must listen to the words as well as the music."

Jakob interrupted. "I know the passage. It was *work heartily as serving the Lord and not men.*"

"Well done," said his father. "The Bible teaches us to do our best for the Lord, and if you do this, Sebastian, someday you will play as skillfully as Christoph does."

They soon reached the Bach home with its red tiled roof and timbered doorway. The house was large enough for their family and the apprentices who lived with them.

Sebastian followed his father up the stairs to the dining room and sat between his two brothers at the long table filled with family and apprentices. His mother and sister brought in a savory stew, and the conversation hummed around him. He felt happiness welling up inside—this was where he belonged.

A hush fell as his father said the blessing. "Come, Lord Jesus, and be our guest. Let Thy gifts to us be blessed."

Sebastian took large bites of a crispy roll while Christoph talked about his teacher. "Herr Pachelbel told me that he knows many musicians from our family."

"That's right," his father replied. "He has been a friend of our family since the days of Great Uncle Heinrich. Today, so many Bachs are musicians, that people expect anyone with the name to play an instrument."

"Tell us about the first Bach," said Jakob. This was an old story, but Sebastian loved to hear it again.

His father leaned back in his chair and took up his pipe. "The first Bach was your great-great-grandfather, Veit the Miller, who played the cittern. He used to play it while he ground the grain, and a pretty noise the mill and cittern made."

"It must have taught him to keep time," added Christoph. He winked at Sebastian who did not always worry about keeping time during his music lessons.

"Veit the Miller went to Hungary for a time and then returned to Germany," continued their father. "He had a son named Hans the Spielmann, who became a famous fiddler. He had three sons, and one of them was your grandfather, Christoph Bach, who played the violin. His two brothers were musicians as well."

"Great Uncle Heinrich is the organist at Arnstadt," said Maria Salome primly. She was proud of the fact that she had gone there once to hear him play.

Sebastian's father held up three fingers. "Each of these three sons had three sons who became musicians, and these are the uncles and cousins who come to family reunions."

Sebastian thought with pleasure of the Bach gatherings and wondered when the next one would be. He had scarcely scooped the last spoonful of stew into his mouth when the meal ended. His father led the family in prayer, as was the custom after each meal: "O give thanks unto the Lord, for He is good: For His mercy endureth forever. Amen."

*****

Today was Sebastian's fifth birthday. His brother Jakob had promised him a treat because at last he was old enough to make the hike to Wartburg Castle. Every day of his life Sebastian had looked from the window of his home and seen the old castle rising on the craggy hill. Sometimes mist wreathed the place like a fairy palace, and other times the dark outlines seemed carved from the very rock of the mountain. He dreamed of scaling the heights like a soldier of old, and now the day had come!

Sebastian followed his brother up the thickly wooded slope. Jakob pushed aside the dense branches and pointed to the castle in the distance. "That is the south tower," he whispered.

A stone structure rose above the tree tops, and the blank windows gave Sebastian an eerie feeling. A single crow, perching on one of the walls, cawed raucously and flapped away.

"Masked men kidnapped Martin Luther and took him there," Jakob whispered.

Sebastian shivered. "What happened to him?"

"They hid him in the castle to protect him from his enemies."

"They didn't put him in the dungeon?"

"No silly—he was a guest, and no one knew his true identity. Every day he disappeared into his room and wrote and wrote. Then one day they saw what he was doing. He was translating the New Testament from Greek into German."

"But I thought the Bible was always in German," said Sebastian.

Jakob gave him a scornful look and forgot to talk in his

hushed voice. "Don't they teach you anything in kindergarten? We learn the Bible in German now, but the New Testament was first written in Greek. A boy in my class has a brother who is going to the university to learn Greek, so he can read the Bible like Martin Luther."

Sebastian, impressed with Jakob's vast knowledge, was thoughtful as they climbed down the mountain. He felt proud when he saw Martin Luther's name as the author of the hymns they sang in church because Eisenach was Luther's hometown. Now it seemed he had done much more than write hymns. Sebastian tried to imagine what it would be like to live in a time when the Bible was not written in German.

*Martin Luther by Lucas Cranach

7

Chapter Two

Qui cantat, bis orat.
(He who sings, prays twice.)
~A precept of St. Augustine taught at the St. George Latin
School

Cousins and Quodlibets

It was harvest time and the Bach family was gathering at Sebastian's home this year. The house was filled with the spicy smell of apple sauce simmering on the stove, and the apprentices were busy moving tables and chairs in preparation.

Sebastian's mother sent him with a note to old Cousin Johann Christoph. He lived on the same street and was helping with preparations for the reunion. When Sebastian knocked at his door there was no answer.

"You will have to take the message to him at the church," said his mother when he returned. "If he is playing the organ, wait quietly until he is finished."

At St. George's Church, Sebastian lingered in the sanctuary while the music swirled around him. He liked the familiar dusty smell of the church and the complicated harmonies the elderly organist wove with his music.

8

Cousin Johann Christoph composed church music not only for the organ, but also for choirs. Sebastian's father liked to remark on the time he wrote a vocal concerto for twenty-two independent voices and instruments. "Not the smallest error in harmony!" he told Sebastian. "I have never heard anything to approach it."

When the music stopped, Sebastian climbed the steps to the organ loft where his cousin greeted him warmly. "Hello, my Sebastian, are you running away from your chores to see your old cousin?"

"Mother asked me to bring you this message, but I was hoping you might let me play the organ with you."

Cousin Johann Christoph pretended to look stern. "What's this I hear about your father teaching you the violin? You are not forgetting all my lessons?"

"Oh no! Papa says that my violin practice will help me learn the organ better."

Cousin Johann Christoph lifted him onto the high seat. "I will play the pedals while you show me what you can play on the keyboard. Then we must go home and help your mother with the rest of the preparations."

The next day Sebastian's Uncle Christoph arrived from Arnstadt. He was an identical twin to Sebastian's father. "I am wearing my red overcoat," he announced as he embraced his brother. "This will help our wives to tell us apart!" He was a music director like his twin brother.

Uncle Christoph brought his sons Johann Ernst and

Johann Christoph with him. They joked that they belonged to the Johann brotherhood because, though they used their middle names, all of them had Johann for a first name. Sebastian's father was Johann Ambrosius, his uncle was Johann Christoph, Sebastian's brothers were Johann Christoph and Johann Jakob, and he was Johann Sebastian. There were also cousins Johann Bernhard, Johann Nikolaus, and Johann Valentin. They looked forward to fun times together at the reunion.

Of the many cousins near his age, Sebastian's favorite was Maria Barbara, whose father was the cousin of Sebastian's father. She came with her father, two older sisters, and her grandfather Heinrich, who was the oldest Bach at the reunion.

Maria Barbara was just a few months older than Sebastian, but she was much smaller. She had curly brown hair and laughing eyes. For some reason that Sebastian could not understand, he always seemed to be in trouble when she was visiting.

"Is is true that your mother is making gingerbread?" she asked the first day as Sebastian and some of the younger cousins clustered around her. "Let's see if she will give us some."

They found the kitchen empty except for the cat curled up by the oven. There was a delicious smell of spices, and on the table lay two round cakes of gingerbread.

"No one will notice if we break off a piece," said Maria

Barbara. Sebastian thought of his mother's strict rules about taking food between meals, but with his cousin's bright eyes on him he could not resist the temptation to show off.

"My mother lets me have treats whenever I like," he said. He reached out to take a piece when suddenly his sister, Maria Salome, came through the door.

"Sebastian," she said in a scandalized voice. "You must never take gingerbread without asking Mother first!" At that moment Maria Barbara's oldest sister Friedelena bustled into the room. She was like a mother to the little girl since their own mother had died. She wagged a finger sternly at her little sister.

Maria Barbara grabbed Sebastian's hand and all the cousins ran from the kitchen, Maria Barbara laughing the whole way. As the shouts of the older sisters faded in the distance, she squeezed his hand. "Never mind, Sebastian. There will be more for dinner!"

Dinner was a grand affair with the families contributing their specialties. Sebastian's mother made her famous baked ham with raisin sauce, and other Bachs brought sour dough bread, baked apples, country vegetables and so many other foods that Sebastian could not try them all. Old Cousin Johann Christoph brought the Eisenach ale, which was part of his payment as town organist. Then there was gingerbread for dessert.

After dinner Sebastian listened as the family sang a sacred chorale together. Next the men began a game of combining well-known melodies into a *quodlibet*. The term *quodlibet* was Latin for "whatever you please." Everyone participated, blending popular songs and old folk tunes into intriguing harmonies that wove in and out of each other.

A glow of happiness filled Sebastian, burning steadily like one of mother's lamps. Surely, being in the midst of a large family was the happiest place to be. He fell asleep to the sound of music and laughter.

The next day his father, uncles and cousins brought out their instruments to play. Many of them crafted their own instruments, and they liked to discuss recent inventions. "Have you seen the new harpsichord?" asked Uncle Georg. "It has a tab of crow quills that plucks the strings."

"I have experimented with leather with good results," added another cousin, and he described a lute-harpsichord that he was creating.

"How about your violins, Michael?" asked Sebastian's father. "I heard that you were perfecting them."

"Indeed, they are getting better. I have just finished a small violin for my daughter Maria Barbara. I think Sebastian could use one as well." He winked at Sebastian who was listening in wide-eyed wonder.

"Sebastian will put it to good use," said his father. "He has received a choral scholarship to the St. George Latin School."

"We are proud of our school," added old Cousin Johann Christoph. "Martin Luther studied there over a hundred years ago. The boys' choir sings with my organ every Sunday in church, and on festival days they sing from house to house."

"Ah, the famous *Currenden* singers," said Michael. He turned to Sebastian. "Are you old enough to sing in the choir?"

Sebastian stood as tall as he could. "I am eight years old now," he said.

"Quite a man," said old Cousin Johann Christoph, and Sebastian wondered why his uncles laughed.

The next week school began. Since Sebastian knew how to read and write, he started in the *quinta* or fifth class. He opened his new text book to the first page and read: "Why do you go to school?" The teacher told them they must memorize and recite the answer: "So that I may grow up righteous and learned."

Sebastian also received a book for Latin. It showed the sentences in German and Latin with interesting illustrations on every page.

The first day in school Sebastian heard a festive tune broke out in the market square. He knew the town musicians played every day at ten o'clock, and he imagined his father leading the band.

For the next few months, Sebastian walked to school with his brother Jakob in the dim light of dawn. Class began at six o'clock in the morning. The teachers dismissed them each day at three o'clock in the afternoon. As the weather became colder and the days grew shorter, school began an hour later. Often darkness had fallen by the time they arrived home.

Sebastian found studying for school similar to learning the violin. He felt an urgency to learn as much as he could. His father admired his progress but worried that he worked too hard. "You don't need to go so fast, son."

Sebastian could not explain the hunger that drove him to learn. "It doesn't seem like work when I study. Please, Papa, don't make me slow down."

After the first semester the headmaster promoted Sebastian to the *quarta* or fourth class with Jakob. The students began to memorize the catechism, which they must learn to become members of the church. They also translated passages from the Latin Bible. Sebastian learned his first prayer in Latin: *Jesu juve*, which meant, *Jesus, help me.*

In addition to school, he had choir rehearsals and violin practice. Whenever his father had time, he gave him a lesson. With music and school, Sebastian learned as fast as he liked, and everyday he hurried home to tell his mother about his school day.

A few months ago, his cheerful mother had become ill. She had to stay in bed, but she always brightened when her youngest son came home. She asked him questions about his lessons and helped him practice his catechism for the next day.

Today she listened while Sebastian read his Bible

assignment aloud.

"Let not your heart be troubled: ye believe in God, believe also in me. In my Father's house are many mansions: if it were not so, I would have told you. I go to prepare a place for you. And if I go and prepare a place for you, I will come again, and receive you unto myself; that where I am, there ye may be also."

His mother had a dreamy look in her eyes. "Remember all that you learn from the Bible, Sebastian. You will find the hope of our faith. Even in death, it gives life meaning." She took his hand and spoke so softly he barely caught her words. "One day you will understand."

The next week Sebastian's mother passed away. His father, with the loss of his wife of twenty-six years, grew old overnight. He no longer came home from an evening playing with his orchestra to regale the children with stories of the festivities. He ate only a few bites of the food that Maria Salome prepared. When he gave violin lessons to Sebastian, he sat quietly looking into space as though he neither saw nor heard his son. Sebastian tried to cheer him with lively tunes, but nothing broke through his despondency.

The months passed. Sebastian was in his second year at the St. George School when his family traveled to Ohrdruf for the wedding of his brother Christoph to Dorothea Vonhoff. Sebastian's father brought a wedding piece composed by old Cousin Johann Christoph called *My Friend, you are Beautiful.* Family and friends supplied the many parts needed for choir and instruments.

His father lost his melancholy at the wedding festivities. "How your mother would have enjoyed seeing Christoph marry so well," he told Sebastian.

At the wedding his father met Dame Barbara Margaretha. She was the widow of a Bach cousin, and she had two young daughters who were close in age to Sebastian and Jakob.

On the way home, his father seemed more cheerful. "I find a great comfort in the friendship of Dame Barbara," he told the boys. "She understands the sadness of losing a spouse." To Sebastian's surprise, a month later they were married. She brought her two daughters, Catharina Margaretha and Christina Maria, to live with the family.

At last Sebastian's father was jovial again. He played lively gigues for the family each evening and told the children stories. Christmas that year was especially joyful.

The family walked through the early morning snow to the church service where Sebastian and Jakob sang in the choir. Their father led the town musicians to the accompaniment of old Cousin Johann Christoph's organ music. Sebastian watched the flickering candlelight play over the faces of the congregation as they sang the traditional Christmas hymns.

After the church service, the family celebrated with a special meal and gifts. Maria Salome admired the collar crocheted for her by Dame Margaretha, and the two younger girls squeaked with pleasure at the lockets presented to them by Sebastian's father. Jakob had a woolen waistcoat, and Sebastian received a book full of creamy white pages. "For you to copy music into," his father told him.

They closed the day singing a Christmas hymn together around the fire. "Glory to God in highest Heaven," sang Sebastian's father in his deep bass.

"Who unto man His Son hath given!" followed the girls with their soft sopranos.

"While angels sing with pious mirth a glad New Year to all the earth," caroled Jakob and Sebastian. After the festive day, full of holy music and family celebration, Sebastian wished that Christmas could continue forever.

Soon after the first of the year, however, Sebastian's father became ill. In February the illness grew worse. The doctor did what he could, but he knew there would be no recovery for his patient.

"He is very sick," he explained to the family. "You must do what you can to make him comfortable." Two months after his marriage, Sebastian's father passed away.

Sebastian's stepmother did not know what to do. She had no means to support the family, and her relatives encouraged her to make her home with them. Sebastian's sister, Maria Salome, was engaged to be married, but the two youngest boys still needed a home. She wrote to Christoph, and they decided that Sebastian and Jakob would go to Ohrdruf to live with him.

Sebastian wondered if Christoph's new wife would like them. Would she mind having two boys in her home? Sebastian was not yet ten, and Jakob was only thirteen.

*Sebastian's father, Johann Ambrosius Bach

Chapter Three

Lord, I trust thee, help my weakness,/Let me, yea, not know despair./Thou, thou canst my strength make firmer/When by sin and death I'm vexed.
~ translation of text used by Johann Sebastian Bach for the closing chorale of the cantata entitled *I Have Faith, O Dear Lord, Help my Unbelieving, BWV 109*

A New Home

On a wintry day, a farmer's cart rumbled slowly on its way to Ohrdruf. The wagon hit a rut in the road, and Sebastian gripped the box that lay across his knees. It contained all he owned—a few suits of clothing, two school books and his Christmas book, already half-filled with music. Another case held his most precious belonging: the violin he had inherited from his father. As he thought of him, a great sadness settled like a blanket on his heart.

The cart came to a halt in front of a small cottage tucked between two larger houses in the shadow of St. Michael's Church. Sebastian helped his brother lift the bags from the back of the wagon and then knocked on the door. They heard the soft metallic notes of a melody played on a clavichord. At the sound of their knock, the music stopped and their brother, grinning broadly, opened the door. His young wife, Dorothea, rushed past him and hugged each boy in turn.

"Welcome, my little ones!" she said.

Their house smelled of freshly baked bread, and Sebastian thought he might like it there.

That evening they gathered around the clavichord, and Christoph invited the boys to join him. While Jakob played a duet with their older brother, Sebastian accompanied them on the violin. The aching notes of music were like a balm for his heart. Sebastian knew he was home.

Sebastian and Jakob went to school at the Lyceum, which lay in the next street. They attended the *tertia* class now, where they learned Latin, arithmetic, history, science, theology and singing. Their cousin Ernst, whose father was the identical twin to their own father, was in their class, and the cousins became choir boys in the church.

Herr Arnold taught the *tertia* class and choir. He was so quick with the cane that the boys did everything they could to avoid catching his attention. Sebastian, with his swift memory, usually avoided his wrath, but Ernst was not so fortunate. The teacher criticized him mercilessly, often caning him for a trivial reason. Since his father had recently died, Ernst boarded at the school. He was ashamed to write to his mother about Herr Arnold.

One day the punishment was worse than usual. Herr Arnold asked Ernst a question about geography, and when he began to stutter his answer, the teacher brought down a ruler on his head. Sebastian was so angry he vowed to do something.

At home that evening Sebastian told his brother about Herr Arnold and how harshly he treated the students. The next day Christoph went to see Headmaster Kiesewetter, who decided to promote Ernst to the *secunda* class for his protection. "And I will be watching Herr Arnold," he promised.

A few days later the headmaster came upon the man viciously caning one of the boys, and he immediately dismissed him from the school.

The new teacher was Herr Herda, fresh from his theological studies at the University of Jena. He soon became one of the favorite teachers among the boys. He admired the hymns by Martin Luther and explained them to the students, waving his arms enthusiastically as he talked.

One day he stopped the choir to tell them about the verses they were singing. "In this hymn, Luther is teaching us that Christians should think of the cross of Christ as both a gift and an example," he said. "We are saved by the cross as a gift, but," and here he shook his finger at the class, "we are also invited to be *like* Christ and take up our cross to follow him."

Sebastian wondered what it would mean for a school boy to take up his cross to follow Christ. In history they learned about the early Christians who died for their faith and the people in Luther's time who fought for what they believed. But what did it mean now?

As the boys began singing the hymn, Sebastian imagined he was marching in a procession made up of believers throughout the ages. There would be barefoot fishermen and strangely garbed people from the countries St. Paul visited. There would be somber monks and dusty stone masons who built the great cathedrals and rugged soldiers of the reformation. Mingling with this great crowd, the students in choir robes would be singing praises to the King of Kings.

Sebastian enjoyed the busy school days, but the happiest times were on Saturday afternoons when Christoph took the boys to help him rehearse on the organ at St. Michael's Church. The church paid a man to work the bellows during services, but the salary did not include time for practice. Christoph found the solution by training his brothers to pump the bellows and keep the wind chest full of air. Rehearsals were long because the church music often lasted over two hours.

"Listen, boys," Christoph said one day, as he played a favorite hymn. "Hear how the organ must be used for a different kind of music from the clavichord. It must be grand. It must fill the space and make the people think of God."

He showed them how to choose and combine the stops of the organ to get the best sound. "You must consider the individual organ and the acoustics of the surrounding space. Listen to this," he said as he changed the stops again and played in a new key.

Sebastian was intrigued. "What would happen if you pulled out all the stops?" he asked.

"It is rather unusual, but here, listen for yourself." He drew out the stops, one after another, and then played a few notes slowly.

"There's a richness about it that I like," said Sebastian.

His brother laughed. "You will be inventing your own way of playing the organ before long!"

Christoph began teaching his brothers on the clavichord in a systematic manner. Though he owned a collection of music by famous composers, he assigned his brothers simple exercises and did not allow them to try the complex music.

Sebastian ached to play like his brother. He hungrily listened to every piece Christoph performed and begged to learn the music, but his brother was firm.

"It's too advanced for you," he said, as he locked the precious music into a latticed cupboard. "If you study it now, you will only learn bad habits."

Sebastian could not resist the appeal of that music. He found if he was careful, he could pull the manuscript from the locked cupboard through the latticework on the front. For the next six months he used every moonlit night to copy the forbidden music.

One evening his brother discovered his secret and took away both the music and the copies. "You will ruin your eyes trying to write in the dark," he scolded him. "I will keep these until you show me that you are wise enough to listen to your older brother."

Soon after this, Jakob reached the age of fourteen and became an apprentice to the town musician who succeeded his father in Eisenach. Sebastian missed his brother, but he comforted himself with the idea that he would finish school as fast as he could and seek an apprenticeship as Jakob did.

By July of 1697 Sebastian was first in his class and was promoted to the *secunda* or second class. He added Cicero's *Letters* and Greek to the subjects he studied. In those days students attended each grade for two years, but Sebastian advanced through the early classes quickly. He was three or four years younger than most of the boys in his grade. Though he was small in stature, he won the respect of his classmates with his singing. He had the ability to stay on perfect pitch, and Herr Herda often assigned him solos to sing in the choir.

His cousin Ernst was in his class again. He introduced Sebastian to a young man named George Erdmann, who also sang solos. He shared a passion for church music with the cousins.

"If I can win a scholarship I want to finish my schooling at one of the great choir schools like Herr Herda attended," he confided to Sebastian and Ernst. "They have music there that we can only dream of here."

One day Sebastian's brother Christoph came home whistling happily. "They are going to re-build the church organ," he announced.

"I thought you considered it a fine organ," said Dorothea.

"It will be even better," he replied.

The next Saturday when Sebastian accompanied his brother to church, he saw the organ being taken apart. From that moment his full attention focused on the instrument. He visited it after school and often missed his dinner in his eagerness to see each detail of the renovation.

The master organ builder was Herr Sterzing. He was a wiry man who seemed to be in every place at once. He took a liking to Sebastian and began saving parts of the contraption to show him. "The organ, young man, is the most complex device ever made by man," he told Sebastian as he pulled out parts from below the keys.

Sebastian had never seen the mechanism inside the organ. Herr Sterzing showed him how the *key action* connected the key to the pipe, and Sebastian watched in fascination, asking questions and picking up each piece as it came from the instrument.

Another day the craftsmen worked on the rows of organ pipes. Sebastian followed their progress as they carefully attached them to the sanctuary wall.

"Each of the pipes plays a single pitch," Herr Sterzing told him. "The longer the pipe, the lower the pitch will be. The tricky part is to adjust the voice just right for the best tone and volume. That's my job."

At last, after many months, Herr Sterzing completed the intricate parts of the organ and began rebuilding the wind system. "It's important to have a good supply of wind so the notes don't die out as they do on your pretty little clavichord," he said.

He patted the wind chest affectionately. "I call these the lungs of the organ. They should be strong enough to make a good sound with all the stops pulled out. You man the bellows and let me show you how it works."

Sebastian began pumping the bellows. He had developed a regular rhythm that allowed him to continue for long periods. "You make a good bellows-worker, son," the builder said.

"I work for my brother," Sebastian said. "We like to practice whenever we can."

"That's a good organist. If you can't afford to pay someone to work the bellows, you have to rehearse on a clavichord, and that's not the same thing at all."

He turned his attention to arranging the organ stops, and before Sebastian was prepared, the first chord from the new organ burst into the sanctuary. Herr Sterzing held it for a long moment then broke into a stately composition of the *Sanctus,* filling the church with glorious tones. "Heaven and earth are full of your glory." The words sang in Sebastian's mind, and the music wove the power of that glory around him.

Chapter Four

The principal cause of God's salvation in word and power is the Gospel, which is the means of salvation. But the meritorious cause is Christ…thus the sinner who believes in Christ is made righteous …The final cause is life and eternal salvation.
~text underlined by Johann Sebastian Bach from the commentary on Romans 1:17 from his *Calov Bible Commentary*

A Choral Scholar

Sebastian was almost fifteen when Herr Herda recommended him and his friend, George Erdmann, as choral scholars to the prestigious St. Michael's School in Lüneburg.

George was thrilled. "We will sing in one of the finest capella choirs in Germany," he told Sebastian. "And think of the education—the school is full of the sons of noblemen, who will have important careers in the government and military when they graduate."

Christoph was proud of his brother's scholarship. "The Bachs have never had such an opportunity," he told him. "You are the first of our family to attain beyond the level of *tertia* in school, and in Lüneburg you will be able to study the grand organs of the north."

Dorothea's father had attended the university. "Papa

says that you will do well to complete your education," she said. "He bids you to greet his friend from university days, Georg Böhm."

Georg Böhm had grown up in a nearby village and later became one of the greatest organists in Germany. The people of Thuringia took pride in his accomplishments.

Sebastian felt some regret at leaving the family that had provided a home for him for the last five years. There were three little nephews now, who worshipped their uncle and cried when they learned he must leave. "When I am done with my studies, I will come back home," he promised them.

The journey to Lüneburg was long. At first the boys walked roads bordering broad pasture lands. They saw farm cottages in the distance with their green shutters and wide red roofs. George kept up a happy chatter, telling Sebastian of all that happened to him since he left school a few months ago.

Soon the way led through a thick forest, and fir cones carpeted the path. Dorothea had packed meat pies and two round loaves for the boys. They found a comfortable spot under an old birch tree for their picnic. The woodland smells blended pleasantly with the yeasty aroma of the fresh bread. A bird trilled in the distance, and Sebastian felt he could write music in a place like this.

"Do you think we will get there in time for Holy Week?" he asked.

George squinted up at the sun, which was beginning its

descent. He was accustomed to hiking home on the holidays from school. "If we can keep the pace, we should be on schedule."

They continued through the forest, and Sebastian started singing a hymn. George joined in with his strong baritone, and when a farmer in his cart rattled by, he offered the boys a ride to the next town. The boys tried to pay him for the help, but he shook his head. "Your payment is your song," he told them.

Over the next seven days Sebastian and George walked ten hours every day, catching rides on farm carts when they could. They passed through villages where flower baskets hung from the beams of balconies and through thick forests where they caught the tangy smell of smoke from the charcoal burners working over their fires.

By the eighth day they reached northern lands where boggy moors, covered with heather, stretched as far as they could see. Cottages were few and the clusters of larch and fir trees were scattered sparsely.

They did not meet any helpful farm carts that day. Their road lay along a deep gully, and they slept in the shadow of an abandoned barn. The long days of walking were beginning to take their toll. Sebastian had blisters on his feet and his stomach felt hollow.

The next day dawned with a drizzly rain, and Sebastian wondered if the moorland would ever end. Even George's spirits seemed dampened. Sebastian tucked his head under his hood and decided to walk forward, keeping his eyes on the ground in front of him. The dampness soaked through to his skin, but the effort of walking kept him warm.

Hours passed and the rain fell steadily. It did not seem worth stopping for a midday meal. Just when Sebastian thought he could not walk another mile, George gave a yell. "The spires of Lüneburg!'

Sebastian peered into the distance. His eyesight was not strong, but he could see a misty hump with pointy projections.

*Detail of Lüneburg from a painting by Hans Bornemann (c. 1450)

With fresh enthusiasm, the boys covered the remaining miles in an hour. As they entered the town gates, the rain stopped and the sun suddenly dazzled on shining rooftops and church towers.

"We're here at last!" said George, thumping Sebastian on the back.

Sebastian looked with wonder at the activity of the crowded streets of Lüneburg. It was one of the chief towns of northern Germany, and loads of merchandise from other ports rumbled past on their way to and from the river docks. Walking along the winding alleys, the boys searched until they found the bell tower of St. Michael's Church. After a journey of two hundred miles, they had reached their goal.

St. Michael's Church was a massive structure with high stone walls and a large courtyard. Drawn by the rich tones of organ music, the boys stepped into the church nave. The voices of a boys' choir filled the sanctuary with piercingly beautiful sound, and Sebastian's weariness fell away.

The choirmaster, a stout man wearing long black robes, saw the two boys lingering in the doorway and beckoned to them.

"Are you come from Herr Herda?" he asked.

"How did you know?" asked Sebastian.

"You look like you've been walking a long way," he replied with a chuckle. "Take your packs to the dormitory and be ready to sing in Matins tomorrow morning."

Sebastian and George had arrived in time for Holy week, and their first week at school was a whirlwind of regular church services and rehearsals for Palm Sunday, Good Friday and Easter. The music was on a larger scale than Sebastian had ever experienced. The music was so absorbing that it was a shock when school began after Easter.

Sebastian was placed in the *prima* or first class taught by the headmaster, Herr Busche. In addition to weighty books on theology, logic and rhetoric, he studied Latin literature including Virgil's *Aeneid* and Cicero's *De Catalina*.

The choirmaster, Herr Braun, lectured on arithmetic, and the assistant to the headmaster instructed the students in Greek using the New Testament. Sebastian remembered Jakob telling him about Martin Luther, who translated the Bible from Greek. Now he was reading it for himself. He also had lessons in physics, French and Italian.

Sebastian enjoyed every minute of his busy days. The school was considered one of the finest choir schools in Germany, and the music was magnificent.

By his third week of school he grew accustomed to the new schedule and his place in the choir. He was singing in the midday rehearsal when suddenly his voice started skipping to unexpected octaves. Within a week he completely lost his treble voice.

The choirmaster frowned with concern. "I'm afraid you will have to supply the bass voice in the Matins choir," he said. Then he brightened. "We need an accompaniment for the larger choir. What instruments do you play?"

"Violin and viola, but I most like to play the organ," Sebastian replied.

"The organ? How did you learn?

"My brother, Christoph Bach, taught me."

The choirmaster nodded with approval. "I've heard of him. Show me what you can play."

Sebastian sat at the organ, a wave of nervousness churning in his stomach. With the first chord of music, however, he forgot everything else. The music lifted him above his worries about losing his voice and filled him with a fresh sense of hope.

The choirmaster was silent for a moment after the short recital. "You must meet my friend Georg Böhm. He will want to hear you."

Sebastian thrilled at the name of Georg Böhm—the man his family wanted him to find in Lüneburg!

The next week the choirmaster himself introduced Sebastian to Herr Böhm. He was organist at the Church of St. John with its famous organ built over a hundred years ago. He was pleased to meet a fellow Thuringian, and inquired after Dorothea's family whom he remembered well. When he heard Sebastian play, he clapped the young man on the shoulder. "You must become my pupil."

In addition to lessons with Herr Böhm, Sebastian played the harpsichord for the choir every day after school. He finished his day with organ practice and then studied in the library before bed. He also rehearsed with a chamber orchestra twice a week.

One day the director of the chamber orchestra rushed into the rehearsal room, flourishing a document decorated with a ribbon and seal. "We have been invited to play at Celle Castle," he said. "They will send a coach to bring us to the concert."

He folded the invitation reverently and placed it on the music stand. "For this performance we must work as we have never worked before. We must shine for the princes at the royal Celle Castle—it is not called *little Versailles* for nothing!"

The next week a richly appointed coach arrived at the school gate. The students, clutching their instruments, sat rigidly on the brocade cushions. Sebastian watched the city of Lüneburg give way to forests and rocky streams. At last the coach rolled up to the castle. Surrounded by pleasure gardens with fountains, the domed towers rose above a façade copied from the palaces of Venice.

A castle official met them at the door and led them past rooms adorned with golden candelabras and velvet curtains.

"You will perform in our new theater," he told them. Sebastian looked with awe at the rows and rows of gilt chairs in the audience.

That night they performed before the noblemen and government officials of the court. Accustomed to performing in church, they were surprised by the thunderous applause that followed their concert.

"We will go home to Lüneburg and tell them we were a success!" declared the director. Sebastian wondered what Christoph would think if he could see him tonight.

Back at school Sebastian worked harder than ever for Herr Böhm. The organ music was beginning to come alive in his mind, and he was eager to find the hidden emotion contained in each piece.

At the end of the lesson one day Herr Böhm asked him

to remain. "Sebastian, the highest purpose of the arts is to serve God, who gave them and created them. This is especially true of music."

This was one of Herr Böhm's favorite themes, so Sebastian nodded in agreement.

"I have been thinking—perhaps the gift you have been given should be used for the service of God," said Herr Böhm. "I want you to think about this."

That evening as Sebastian participated in the evensong service, he considered his teacher's words. The robes of the student choir glowed red in the flickering candlelight. Their voices rose in fluid harmonies singing praise to God as the choirmaster directed them from his place at the front. "Is this where I am meant to serve one day?" Sebastian wondered. He was still deep in thought as the blessing was spoken and the students sang the final amen.

Sebastian thought about Herr Böhm's words while he studied from the huge collection of sacred music in the school library. As he read the compositions, he listened with delight as they played in his head. He found motets by his own relations, Great Uncle Heinrich and old Cousin Johann Christoph. He copied many of them and brought them to Herr Böhm.

Herr Böhm encouraged Sebastian to learn from other musicians and was pleased with the new music he brought. "This reminds me of my old professor," he said. "He is Adam Reinken, the renowned organist in Hamburg. He is still performing at the age of seventy."

Herr Böhm sat at the organ and began playing a piece of music that flowed with layer upon layer of rich tones. He paused. "Reinken taught me that organ music must be solemn and majestic to suit the holy purpose of the place. You must give the echoes liberty to rise and slowly die away in the spaces of the church. Listen again."

As Sebastian listened, the music changed form in his mind. "The echoes are part of the music!" he said.

Herr Böhm smiled with approval. "Try the chorale by your great Uncle Heinrich and let the echoes rise into the very dome of the sanctuary."

The more Sebastian learned of Reinken, the more determined he became to hear him. When the students had a short holiday, he went to the prefect with his request.

"I need permission to leave school to hear Reinken," he told him.

The prefect was doubtful of the wisdom of this venture. "It's thirty miles to Hamburg. Can you get back to school in time?"

"If I can have two days, I can easily return before evensong."

"You may have permission," the older boy said reluctantly. "But don't think you can miss the next choir rehearsal because your feet are sore."

After the long journey to Lüneburg, the hike to Hamburg seemed light. Sebastian started before dawn and arrived by early afternoon.

The music by Reinken put Sebastian in a kind of ecstasy. The organ at St. Catharine's Church was immense, with fifty-eight stops on four manuals and a pedal. Reinken kept them in the best tune of any instrument Sebastian had ever heard. The organ played evenly and on pitch, even down to the lowest C.

Sebastian never thought to introduce himself to the master organist. With the music still playing in his head, he began the long walk home in a daze.

* Johann Adam Reinken playing the harpsichord in a painting by Jan Voorhout 1674

He could not complete the journey that day since the concert ended in the late afternoon. He stopped outside an inn, and felt in his pocket for his few groschen. Unfortunately he did not have enough to pay for a meal. The smell of beef stew and freshly baked bread wafted through the window. He sat below it and wondered if he could feast on the smell itself. It would do no harm to rest there for a moment.

Suddenly the wooden shutter of the window banged open, and the heads of two herrings sailed through the window. They fell on the clean grass in front of Sebastian, and he hungrily picked them up. To his astonishment, each fish head held a shiny Danish ducat.

When he arrived home, his friends crowded around him to hear the story of his trip. They wanted to touch the ducats for themselves. "What will you do with the money?" asked George.

"I'll use it to go back to Hamburg and hear more of Reinken," declared Sebastian.

Sebastian wrote to his family about all that he was learning and about the master organist in Hamburg. To his surprise his cousin Ernst came to Hamburg to study the organ the following April. He remained for six months, and Sebastian stayed with him when he visited Hamburg for recitals. Ernst brought news of the family and their school in Ohrdruf. "Dorothea wants me to tell you that her oldest boy has started learning the violin to be like his Uncle Sebastian, and Headmaster Kiesewetter bids you greetings."

The cousins often shared compositions they were

writing in the style of Reinken. The master organist wrote two-part chorales in which either voice could become the upper or lower voice. "It's like weaving a melody from sound," Sebastian told his cousin.

He showed him the notes he had taken from a manual on the science of organ building by Andreas Werckmeister. The school library contained one precious copy. Ernst shook his head. "There are some things that are too complicated for me."

Sebastian studied the principles taught in the book until he had a thorough grasp of the terms and methods used among organ builders. At his next lesson with Herr Böhm he asked him about the book.

"Ah, Werckmeister—he is a musical scientist!" said Herr Böhm.

"What do you think of his idea of a well-tempered organ?"

Herr Böhm sighed. "Most of our organs are very old. They were not built for such a thing."

"But it could be done?"

"Anything is possible with great effort," his teacher said.

Sebastian could not get the idea of a well-tempered organ out of his mind. It would mean tuning the instrument with all the keys in tune. In the current system some keys sounded out of tune because they contained many notes raised or lowered a half tone. Sebastian hoped he could try Werckmeister's system one day.

With his quest for knowledge, physics became one of Sebastian's favorite classes. The professor regarded science as a type of rule of the universe which pointed to the majesty of God. When he taught about Pythagoras, he explained that the ancients understood music as the natural harmony of the spheres. He made diagrams to show why acoustics worked and how the planets moved. One day he lectured on the solar year.

"This past year our country adopted the Gregorian calendar," he began.

There was a general grumble from the students, who thought the change had been a nuisance.

"Yes, you went to sleep Sunday night, February eighteenth, and woke up Monday morning, March first. I'm surprised you did not receive demerits for such a long nap."

He looked pointedly at George who appeared to be falling asleep already. "The reason for this necessary change can be easily understood if you study our solar year." He jabbed a pointer at the solar diagram at the front of the classroom. "The Julian calendar assumed the solar year was 365.25 days, but in fact it was exactly eleven minutes shorter.

"Every four hundred years we lost three days, and over hundreds of years they accumulated until by the time of Pope Gregory XIII we were ten days behind the solar calendar. He decreed by Papal Bull that the calendar should be changed, but the Protestant countries ignored him for a hundred years."

He tapped lightly on George's desk. "How many minutes were lost during that time, George?"

George snapped to attention just in time.

"Eleven hundred minutes," Sebastian hissed in his ear. He duly repeated this and received a gratified smile from the professor.

"Thus, we adopted the Gregorian calendar so the first day of spring would be restored to its rightful place and the date for Easter would be correct. And now I must dismiss you to your choirmaster, who has much to say about the celebration of Easter this year."

Chapter Five

For thee, Lord, is my desire…
All my days, which pass in sadness
God will end, at last, in gladness.
~Johann Sebastian Bach in *For Thee, Lord, is my Desire*, BWV
150
Bach's earliest surviving cantata

Arnstadt

It was January of 1703, and Sebastian had never seen a colder winter. He had graduated at Easter after two years of study at St. Michael's School and stayed on in Lüneburg as accompanist to the choir. Unfortunately his pay was not enough to keep his room heated. He wore a coat indoors and wrapped a blanket around himself as well.

As he peered from his frosted window, the only people stirring in the town were the foresters who strode purposefully through the snowy streets with their guns on their shoulders.

A knock sounded on the front door below, and Sebastian heard someone stamping snow from heavy boots. The next moment George burst into the room waving a letter in his mittened hand. "The choirmaster bade me bring this to you. Open it at once!"

Sebastian sighed. The last letter contained a rejection of

his application for the organist post at Sangerhausen. Yet, when he looked at the seal on the envelope, his mouth grew dry. It was the seal of the house of Duke Johann Ernst. He ruled as co-regent with his brother Wilhelm Ernst of the duchy of Saxe-Weimar. Working at their palaces in Weimar would bring him closer to his family. In addition, Duke Johann Ernst supported the musical arts. Though the court at his Red Palace was small, he often invited prominent musicians to perform there.

Carefully, Sebastian broke the seal and studied the flowery script of the letter.

"What is it?" George asked.

A glow seemed to work through Sebastian from his fingertips to his feet. "I have been appointed court musician in the chapel of the duke!"

George thumped him on the back. "We must tell Herr Böhm. He will be proud to know that one of Lüneburg's students will perform in court."

The duke and his musicians welcomed Sebastian to Weimar. Many of them knew members of his family. Sebastian's skills with the violin and organ also earned their respect.

During the next few months, his reputation as an organist spread. His brother Christoph invited him to play the organ in nearby Ohrdruf.

"I'm impressed with the progress you've made in Lüneburg," he said. "Your pedal work has improved, and you have a polished style on the keyboard."

"I have a gift for you from Lüneburg as well." Sebastian brought out a thick packet of music. "These compositions are by the master, Reinken, and this is one of the most haunting pieces you will ever hear. It is by Herr Böhm who taught me in Lüneburg."

His brother turned over each page, running his eyes along the lines of music. "This is an amazing collection-- Lully and Marchand as well! How did you acquire so many French pieces?"

"Our orchestra leader was fond of French music, and these were part of our repertoire."

"You have put your studies to good use," Christoph said. "I will do all I can to help you find a post as organist."

When St. Boniface Church in nearby Arnstadt needed an organist, Christoph recommended his brother as an excellent candidate. A few weeks later the church invited Sebastian to give the first recital on their new organ.

Before the recital, Sebastian visited the streets of Arnstadt. His father's twin brother had been director of the town musicians there, and he remembered warm visits with his family. He breathed in the smell of fresh bread from the bakery and listened to the rhythmic hammering of the smithy. It was good to be back.

He also visited the Feldhaus home, where his second cousin Maria Barbara lived. She was the same kind, cheerful friend he remembered from the Bach family reunions. Like

44

Sebastian, she had been orphaned when she was nine years old. She now lived with her two older sisters, Friedelena and Catharina, at the home of their aunt and uncle. He invited them to attend the recital.

That evening Sebastian put all his effort into creating a majestic sound from the instrument. The organ was tuned with the new "well-tempered" system that Sebastian had studied in Werckmeister's book, and he admired the effect. He gloried in the physical work of pressing the stiff keys, pulling the heavy stops, and depressing the pedals with his feet while the music swelled around him.

As the last notes died away, the audience exploded with excited comment. He came down from the organ loft, and the rector shook his hand warmly while a crowd pressed around him to give their congratulations.

Sebastian looked for Maria Barbara but did not see her until he was about to leave. She was waiting for him by the church door. "Your father would have been proud," she said shyly.

Sebastian walked home, cheered by the success of his first recital, but most of all, relishing the words of Maria Barbara.

In July the church offered Sebastian the post of organist. He had complete responsibility of the organ from performance to maintenance. In addition to Sunday worship, there were early services two mornings each week and vesper services on Wednesday afternoons.

He found a boy named Johann Caspar Vogler who was willing to work the bellows in return for music lessons. With the extra rehearsal time, Sebastian could experiment and discover how much music he could create. As Sebastian practiced, he savored the layers of sound that flowed from the organ. Surely, music must have been designed to point us to God, he thought.

Sebastian also conducted mid-week choir rehearsals, which soon became his greatest challenge. Most of his students tried to learn, but a single prank could ruin an entire practice. Herr Braun, the choir prefect, could not control the students. Sebastian tried his best, but he was only nineteen years of age, scarcely older than the choir boys. As the weeks passed, however, the choir improved, and the boys began to take pride in their music.

One afternoon Sebastian was rehearsing the student choir. They sang, "*Nunc dimittis servum tuum, Domine, secundum verbum tuum in pace.*"

Sebastian let the meaning of the words roll over him: *Now let your servant depart, Lord, in peace according to your word....* The harmonies began to grow when suddenly two of the singers hit wrong notes and the rest of the group warbled to a stop.

Sebastian sighed. "We will try again from *Domine*. Please hold the last note for the full count."

Sebastian heard a snigger from the back, and suddenly an enormous toad jumped out of the choir loft. The younger

46

boys shrieked and two of the big boys jumped over the front row to capture the toad. By the time the uproar had quieted down, choir rehearsal was over. Sebastian hoped they would perform better at the worship service.

Feeling discouraged with his choir, he made his way to the Feldhaus home for a warm meal and a visit with Maria Barbara.

"How are the boys behaving?" she asked. Her smile curved up on one side as it did when she was teasing.

"They are sounding less like a bunch of donkeys braying," he said. "In fact, I might say there is only one donkey left in the choir."

He told her about the toad incident, and her musical peals of laughter made Sebastian laugh too. Suddenly he saw the humorous side of the rehearsal.

Maria Barbara wiped the tears of laughter from her eyes. "You will transform them, Sebastian. Never fear."

Sebastian spent the rest of the evening playing folk tunes on the clavichord while Maria Barbara and her sisters sang with the music.

"What are you doing with your fingers?" asked Friedelena after his first song. "It's different from the way my father taught me."

"I'm developing a new fingering system for the organ," he said. "Most organists play with flat hands, but I've found that by curving my fingers I can use the thumb and little finger as well."

"I've never seen fingers fly so fast," Maria Barbara said with admiration.

The next week a distant cousin, Johann Ludwig Bach, visited Sebastian. He told him about a set of cantata texts he set to music at his court in Saxe-Meiningen.

"The cantata is replacing the church music used to follow the gospel lesson," he said. "You should try it for your congregation."

He told Sebastian about a pastor named Eerdmann Neumeister. "He began writing poetry for cantatas four years ago. His verses are more like the Italian madrigals— very expressive and spiritual."

Sebastian studied his cousin's compositions. "I'd like to try this, and I notice you have added the Bible text and hymns to the cantata."

"It makes a seamless flow of worship," Ludwig said.

Sebastian worked on his first cantata, but his progress in composition was slow. He often discussed the challenges with Maria Barbara. One afternoon he sat with her in the Feldhaus living room while she worked on her mending.

"I don't see why you are dissatisfied with your compositions," she said. "Your Easter cantata was beautiful. Friedelena talked for days about the words to the closing poem—victory over death."

"The poetry was fine, but I'm afraid my dull composition marred the work."

She laid down her sewing. "Let me see what you have."

Sebastian shuffled the papers. "Perhaps it would be better if I played it for you."

She came to stand behind him and listened while he played on the clavichord. It was a light tune, well-suited to his nimble fingers. "It's lovely," she said when he finished. "But I can't understand your notation."

"I'm experimenting with the new staff notation. It's easier to use than recording the pitch with letters. Each of these spaces and lines represents a note."

Maria Barbara's eyes lit up in comprehension. "How clever. You can actually see the music moving along the page."

"I'm studying the best music I can find so that I can improve my own composition."

"If you keep studying, you will do it," she said.

As he walked home, Sebastian thought about Maria Barbara. In the past few weeks, they had begun to talk about their future. If he could find a position that paid enough for a family, he could ask her to marry him. However, Sebastian knew he would have to grow in his powers as an organist first.

At this time Sebastian's brother Jakob entered the service of the King of Sweden as an oboist in the royal army. Sebastian wrote him a capriccio in B flat which he called *Departure of a Beloved Brother*. Through music he told the fanciful story of a brother departing while his friends try to persuade him to stay. They warn him of the calamities that might happen to him, but he does not listen. The piece ends with a fugue imitating the horn of the postal coach as it carries the brother away. Sebastian dressed up the composition with Latin and Italian subheadings and notes, in imitation of the grand masters.

When Jakob visited to say farewell, he admired the calligraphic copy Sebastian presented to him. "It is a delicate little composition," he said. "You are surely the most dexterous composer I've ever met. May the Lord protect me from such as you in the Royal Swedish Army!"

"You should see the capriccio I wrote in honor of Christoph," Sebastian replied merrily.

Chapter Six

Give unto the LORD the glory due unto his name: bring an offering,
and come before him: worship the LORD in the beauty of holiness.
~I Chronicles 16:2

Evening Music

Sebastian locked the wooden door of St. Boniface Church and put the heavy brass key in his pocket. The choir still needed improvement, but two years of hard work had resulted in good progress.

A soft wind blew the smell of newly mown hay from the fields outside of town. Sebastian paused to watch the late summer sun setting over the Old City, with its quaint mixture of red tile roofs and Romanesque towers. As he walked down the main street, he contemplated his newest composition, a toccata and fugue in D minor. He liked composing fugues because he could create different parts that chased each other through the music. He considered ending it with a passage of paired chords, played so each pair became a little lower than the one preceding it.

In the middle of his musings, an elderly gentleman hailed him. He was concertmaster to Count Anton Gunther II.

*St. Boniface Church, Arnstadt

The count had great respect for the Bach family. When Sebastian was ten years old, the count lost his court musician who was a relative of Sebastian. He wrote to Sebastian's step-mother asking "whether there was not another Bach available, for he must have a Bach again." Sebastian's father had just passed away and the grieving widow wrote in reply: "But this was not to be, for the dear God has caused the springs of musical talent in the Bach family to run dry within the last few years."

When Sebastian came to Arnstadt, the count was thrilled to have a Bach in his community once again. He often invited Sebastian to take part in special entertainments with the court orchestra, and in this way the concertmaster and Sebastian became good friends.

He was a cheerful man, and he seemed especially delighted today. "Sebastian, I have arranged for a famous soprano to visit the court. She will be singing there for several evening performances, and the count asks if you would like to invite her to sing with the choir for the worship service on Sunday."

Sebastian hesitated. His choir was improving, but was it good enough to accompany a guest performer? On the other hand, he dreamed of being able to offer something of this caliber in the worship service. "We would be honored to have her sing," he replied.

The next Sunday the congregation was amazed to hear a voice like an angel coming from the choir loft. Many of the people said the music was superb, but some of them were offended.

A council member confronted Sebastian. "We have never had a woman sing in church. You should have asked permission first."

Sebastian took his worries to Maria Barbara. "I thought the approval of the count was sufficient," he told her.

He looked so miserable that Maria Barbara laughed. "I suppose you imagined the congregation would thank you and tell you what an honor you brought upon Arnstadt," she said teasingly. "Sebastian, not everyone sees great music as the main point in life!"

"But if they did, they would agree that hosting such fine music at our church must glorify the Lord."

"Perhaps they would, but then again perhaps not." She looked at him with the same bright eyes that induced him to steal the gingerbread long ago.

Sebastian chuckled. "Perhaps I am just a ridiculous musician who thinks he knows best without the advice of others."

"Perhaps," Maria Barbara said, kissing him on the cheek.

One evening Sebastian was walking home from a performance at the castle with his cousin Catharina Bach. She was the sister of Maria Barbara and had offered to help the orchestra with the music. Sebastian wore his court uniform with his ceremonial sword at his side. They chatted as they walked through the market square, with its large stone called the Langenstein. It was a popular meeting place, and Sebastian idly noted some young men there now.

Suddenly one of them lurched towards him, waving a stick and shouting. "Bach! I know it is you!"

Sebastian peered through the growing dusk, and then sighed with relief. It was only Geyersbach, the student with the awful bassoon.

"Geyersbach, if you are drunk, the council will hear of it," Sebastian said.

At the sound of Sebastian's voice, the young man grew more excited. He pointed his stick at Sebastian. "You have been abusing my name!"

"Where would you get such an idea?" Sebastian asked.

Geyersbach narrowed his eyes. "It is not myself, but my bassoon you have maligned … once."

Sebastian turned to go, but Geyersbach lunged forward and struck him with his stick. When Sebastian swiveled around to face him, the young man fell on him, wrestling him to the ground. Sebastian smelled the stale wine on his breath and felt Geyersbach shaking with an uncontrollable rage.

With a mighty effort he rolled so that Geyersbach was underneath him. Sebastian pinned the young man's arms firmly to his side while the other students rushed to restrain their friend.

Geyersbach still muttered threats as the young men led him away. Sebastian, feeling shaken, escorted Catharina home in silence. He wondered if the other student musicians felt insulted when he found fault with their instruments or their music. Geyersbach was not a bad musician, but he did need a better instrument. Sebastian realized he must learn how to help students improve without making enemies of them.

Despite the controversy over the guest singer, Count Anton Gunther II remained a great supporter of Sebastian's work. One afternoon he visited the church to listen to him play the organ in preparation for the Sunday worship service. The music expanded until it filled the church, layer upon layer of solemn and thrilling tones that made a rich tapestry of sound. The count climbed the steps to the organ loft and congratulated him on the magnificent music he brought forth from the organ.

"You will be one of the greatest organists of our day, my lad. We must think how we can find a mentor for you."

Sebastian had a proposal, but he worried that it might be too bold.

"Dietrich Buxtehude will perform the *Abendmusiken* at his church in Lübeck," Sebastian began.

"The very idea!" exclaimed the count. "You must present yourself to this organist and tell him you want to learn everything you can. I will write an introduction for you."

The count disappeared as quickly as he had appeared. Sebastian was left wondering how he would get permission from the church to leave his post, and even more important, how he would cover the 250 miles to Lübeck.

To Sebastian's surprise the permission came within a week. The count simply informed the church officers that their organist would be taking a sabbatical. Sebastian arranged for his cousin Ernst to substitute for him. Though autumn was rapidly approaching, the weather remained fair, and Sebastian prepared for his journey. He decided to walk the 250 miles to Lübeck.

On his last night in Arnstadt he visited Maria Barbara. "I will only be away for five weeks," he said. "This may be the opportunity I have been looking for to better myself." He did not say all that he hoped, but he knew a better position meant they could marry and make a home of their own.

* Dietrich Buxtehude from detail of a painting

When Sebastian presented his letter from the count, he received a warm welcome from Herr Buxtehude. His household was full of people and music. He and his wife had six daughters, as well as his brother who lived with them. Sebastian joined the family for impromptu concerts on the clavichord and various stringed instruments. Herr Buxtehude also invited him to play in the large ensemble for the *Abendmusiken*, since he needed a violin player.

The *Abendmusiken* was a Christmas tradition in Lübeck.

The town merchants paid for the concerts, and the entire community attended. Herr Buxtehude composed elaborate oratorios to be performed over the five weeks of celebration.

For the first performance, St. Mary's Church was decorated lavishly. Candles glowed from candelabras and chandeliers. Both large organs were used, as well as two choirs and forty instrumentalists, arranged in groups in various galleries. The concert opened with two bands of trumpets. Sebastian bent over his bow in the orchestra gallery, where he played with twenty-four other violinists. The splendor of the music was a new experience for him.

For the last piece the entire congregation joined in singing. Sebastian thought the combination of organ and vocal performance was sublime.

The next day Herr Buxtehude invited Sebastian to play the organ in St. Mary's Church. He started Sebastian on the smaller organ, but quickly ushered him to the larger instrument, listening spellbound as Sebastian performed.

When he finished, Herr Buxtehude rushed forward and embraced him. "You must stay and become my assistant."

The next five weeks was one of the happiest times in Sebastian's life. Herr Buxtehude took him everywhere with him and introduced him to other musicians who had traveled to Lübeck to perform in the concerts.

When Herr Buxtehude performed, Sebastian felt that he was receiving months of instruction in a single evening. The organist had developed a pedal technique that impressed

Sebastian. In addition, he used a musical architecture in his work that was ten times larger than the work by other composers.

During the day Sebastian would ask Herr Buxtehude why he composed certain sections as he did. The older man would bring out his musical scores to show him. "You must organize your composition on a larger scale—improvise the preludes, yes, but limit the complexity of the counterpoint. Like this…" For his part, Herr Buxtehude was pleased with the dedication and skill of his young friend.

Though the *Abendmusiken* ended, a snow storm blew in, making it impossible for Sebastian to journey home. In the back of his mind he wondered if the council would be angry that he did not return as promised, but he told himself the weather was too severe. Even if he tried to post a letter, it would not get through the snow. Instead he let himself enjoy the enforced stay. He was brimming with ideas for the new style of music. He hoped the organist would formalize the offer of assistantship. It could mean that his plans to marry Maria Barbara would finally come to pass.

One day Herr Buxtehude asked Sebastian to walk with him to the church to get ready for the evening service. As they walked, Herr Buxtehude told him about his life.

"My father was a gifted organist in his day," he began. "He taught me from a young age, and I worked in various churches before I came here." As they turned the corner, he paused to look up at the grand edifice of St. Mary's Church.

"I have served in this church for thirty-five years, and it has been a wonderful place for a musician. Lübeck is a free imperial city, and the musicians have great freedom to compose as they would like."

They reached the church door, and Herr Buxtehude ushered Sebastian inside. He put his hand on the young man's shoulder, and his tone became serious. "When I inherited the post from Herr Tunder, I married his daughter, and we have been very happy here. We would wish the same for you—to marry our oldest daughter and spend your life here."

Sebastian was startled. "Is this a requirement for the post as your assistant?"

"It is the way it has always been done." Herr Buxtehude spread his hands in a gesture that took in not only the church but the city of Lübeck as well.

Sebastian saw his plans for advancement suddenly evaporate. "I am sorry, Herr Buxtehude, but I hope to marry a young woman back home. I cannot consider your kind offer."

Herr Buxtehude was grieved with Sebastian's choice, but he remained firm that his successor must marry his daughter.

Soon the weather cleared and Sebastian took his leave of Herr Buxtehude and his family. "Remember what you have learned here," the organist said, warmly shaking his hand.

Sebastian knew he would never forget.

When Sebastian arrived home in Arnstadt, the church

authorities were angry about his prolonged absence. Nor did they like the new style he brought with him. They complained that the preludes for the hymns confused the congregation with their curious variations.

"If you play the traditional prelude in this way, how will the people know how to sing?" one of the council members said. Other members added their own criticisms.

Sebastian realized too late that he should have handled his tardiness at the *Abendmusiken* better. Now he had made an enemy of the council. The time had come to look for a new post, but first there was something important he needed to do.

As he walked to the Feldhaus home, Sebastian was anxious. Did Maria Barbara still share his plans for the future? The moment he entered the door of the modest cottage, however, he felt at home. They eagerly listened to his report on the progress of his work with Herr Buxtehude.

They talked through the evening, and Sebastian marveled again how easy it was to talk to Maria Barbara and her family. As the early stars began twinkling in the sky, he asked Maria Barbara if she would take a walk with him in the garden.

"There is something important I need to ask you," he said, taking her tiny hand in his own. "If I can get a post that will support a family, will you marry me?"

Maria Barbara laughed. "Of course, dear Sebastian."

Chapter Seven

Holy Scripture plainly says/ That death is swallowed up by death,/ Its sting is lost forever.
~translation of hymn used by Johann Sebastian Bach for his early Easter cantata: *Christ Lay in Bondage to Death,* BWV 4 (perhaps 1708)

Uncle Tobias

As the new leaves of spring began to appear, Maria Barbara's promise gave Sebastian renewed vigor for his work. In addition to his duties at Arnstadt, he applied himself to composition and accepted every offer to test organs or perform for other churches.

During his travels he often stopped by the home of his elderly uncle, Tobias Lammerhirt. On one of his visits to his uncle, Sebastian met his distant cousin, Johann Gottfried Walther. Their mothers were Lammerhirt cousins from Erfurt. The two young men found they had much in common. Both were musicians and composers. Both enjoyed musical puzzles and challenges.

The young men played music for their aunt and uncle, and Uncle Tobias admired a cantata Sebastian was writing called *God's Time is the Best Time.*

"I can hear the steps of our Savior on his way to the cross in the slow deep notes of the music," he said.

Sebastian worked on this composition for several months and added verses from the Old and New Testament as well as hymns. He wrote the cantata for a small ensemble: two alto recorders, a bass continuo and two viola de gambas. In his mind he could hear the soprano, alto, tenor and bass voices blending with the tenor singing "Lord, teach us to consider…" and then the soprano singing "Yes, come, Lord Jesus, come!" and then the alto and bass voices singing "With peace and joy I depart."

The cantata ended with "Glory, praise, honor and majesty" sung with a lively tempo. Uncle Tobias asked him to play this part for him every time he visited, and he would sing along in his piping tenor.

In April, St. Blaise's Church in Mühlhausen invited Sebastian to audition for the post of organist. He performed one of the cantatas he had been writing over the past year, and by June the church offered him the position. At last he could marry Maria Barbara! They began to make their plans, waiting until he earned enough in his new job to set the wedding date.

Soon after Sebastian moved to Mühlhausen, he learned that Uncle Tobias had died. He used the cantata that his uncle had loved for his funeral, remembering with fondness how Uncle Tobias used to sing "Make us triumph through Jesus Christ, our Lord, Amen."

Uncle Tobias left Sebastian and his brothers and sister a modest inheritance. It provided the money Sebastian needed to set up a home with Maria Barbara. They were married on October 17th by their friend Pastor Stauber under the rough-hewn pillars of the country church at Dornheim.

Sebastian's brother Christoph, with Dorothea and their five boys, came to the wedding. The nephews sat on the front row and cheered when Uncle Sebastian walked down the aisle. Bach cousins from near and far came as well. They made their merry music and even improvised a quodlibet on a wedding theme at the marriage breakfast. There were Bernhard from Eisenach, Nikolaus from Jena, and Valentin from Schweinfurt. Ernst from Arnstadt was there, too.

They joked about the early days at Bach family reunions when they schemed to steal the gingerbread. Now the young men had grown into accomplished musicians in their own communities.

Sebastian and Maria Barbara set up their first home in a cottage on the fringe of Mühlhausen. Sebastian took his new wife to see the church soon after they arrived. Together they wandered through the grand building, which was older and more ornate than his last church. The ancient windows glowed with rich colors, and the stone arches soared above the organ loft

"The rector told me that a church has stood on this site since 1227," Sebastian said, as he led her up to the bell tower.

"And look at the bell," she said. "It has a casting mark from 1281."

She joined him in the organ loft as he tested the organ, drawing out all the stops. He piled up notes until they resonated majestically in the airy spaces of the sanctuary.

"You will create sacred music here," she said with a happy sigh.

A soft footstep sounded from the stairs, and a man entered the organ loft. "I heard your music as I passed by and wanted to introduce myself. I'm Pastor Eilmar from St. Mary's Church."

"I look forward to meeting your organist," Sebastian said. "I understand that we will work together to supply music for the other churches and schools."

"He will be glad to meet you as well," Pastor Eilmar said. "Last year fire destroyed a large part of our town, and we're doing what we can to rebuild town spirit. This has kept our organist very busy."

Pastor Eilmar became a close friend. He often sat in the organ loft while Sebastian rehearsed the parts of the Lutheran worship service. One day he listened in his usual posture of prayer as Sebastian played the *Kyrie*. It was a prayer of "Lord have mercy," which traditionally opened the church service. Next Sebastian played the *Gloria* which was a song of praise to the Lord.

"This is the purest kind of worship," he said softly. "Martin Luther once said that the purpose of liturgy is to teach us what we need to know about Christ. I have learned much today."

One day he came to Sebastian with a special request. "The town council wants a cantata for their inauguration ceremony."

"I know the perfect text," Sebastian said. "We can use *God is my King!*"

The pastor smiled with appreciation. "The very thing to remind all earthly governors that God is the king above all rulers."

The two men worked together to prepare the cantata, which they based on Psalm 130 with two hymn stanzas added. Sebastian knew the congregation would like the hymns because their familiarity would appeal to their hearts.

As he composed the music, he realized that his brilliant flourishes without a plan led nowhere. He began to see how a work of music must be carefully shaped from the beginning. As he explained to Maria Barbara: "It's too easy for me to be a finger composer and let my fingers tell me what to write." His hard work began to bear fruit, and he was pleased to see that his compositions were improving.

The following February the cantata was performed for the inauguration. The organist from St. Mary's Church played the organ while Sebastian directed the choir and instruments. The Mühlhausen council was greatly impressed. At the reception afterwards, one councilman promised that the council would publish the cantata. "A great work of art must be appreciated by a wider audience," he declared.

Sebastian shared his triumph with Maria Barbara back in their cottage. As the kettle sang on the stove, Maria Barbara laughed with glee to think of her Sebastian being recognized by the Mühlhausen Council. "This will be only the beginning," she said.

Her prediction came true. The parishioners were so proud of their new organ master that they approved Sebastian's proposal to renovate the organ.

Through his work with the local churches and other public festivities, Sebastian made many friends in the musical community. He had so many opportunities to perform, that he realized he needed more help. He took on his first apprentice that spring. His name was Johann Martin Schubart, but everyone called him Martin. He was five years younger than Sebastian and had studied music for ten years.

Sebastian began by teaching Martin his new fingering for the keyboard. "You must avoid playing as though your fingers were glued together," he said. "Too often the musician depresses the keys too long and the touch is too deliberate."

He demonstrated how this would sound on the clavichord. "At the same time you must not play too crisply, as if the keys burned your fingers." His fingers tripped carelessly over the keys as he illustrated the other extreme to avoid.

When Sebastian showed Martin how to place his hand

on the keys, Martin was startled. "Even the thumb?"

Sebastian laughed. "God gave us thumbs, so we will use them for His music."

Martin shook his head in doubt. In all the years he had studied music, no one had ever taught him to use his thumbs.

Sebastian noticed his hesitation. "Do you see how I can curl my fingers so that they are close to the notes I wish to strike?"

Martin placed his hands in the traditional position with fingers stiff, and Sebastian gently lifted his palm until the fingers curled lightly above the keys. Martin tried a few notes and a slow smile spread across his face. "My fingers don't fall accidentally against the keys."

"Yes, yes! You have discovered a new control," said Sebastian. "Now maintain a uniform pressure and after you strike the note, draw the finger gently toward the palm of your hand."

Martin tried sliding his fingers over the keys and found he could coordinate each finger better. At the end of the hour lesson he wriggled his fingers. "My hands are not tired," he said.

As Sebastian supervised the young man's progress in the days that followed, he realized that Martin's prior training taught him to rely on his stronger fingers. As a result, some compositions were almost impossible for him to play correctly. He invented exercises for him that required the fingers of both hands to practice in every possible position. Martin's fingers soon became strong enough to play a rapid series of chords and running passages with delicacy.

Sebastian's reputation as an organist spread throughout the region. A year after Sebastian took his new post, Duke Wilhelm Ernst invited him to inaugurate the renovated organ at the Wilhelmsburg Palace in Weimar. As Sebastian's hands went one direction, and his feet sped nimbly over the pedals the other way, the duke marveled at Sebastian's skill. He immediately offered him the position of chamber musician and court organist.

Sebastian went to Pastor Eilmar for advice. "This post would give me a patron while I work on church music," he told his friend.

"You must also consider your family," Pastor Eilmar said. "You have fruitful work here, but this new position comes with twice your current salary. As your family grows, you will need this kind of support."

After careful deliberation, Sebastian decided to accept the post. In his resignation letter to the council at Mühlhausen he wrote:

> It has been my constant aim to accord with your desire that church music should be so performed as to exalt God's glory, and, as far as my humble ability has allowed, I have assisted that purpose also in the villages, where the taste for music is growing....If in the future I can be further useful to your church, I can

promise, so long as life is granted me, to show my willingness in deeds no less than words.

Your most obedient servant,
Joh. Seb. Bach
Mühlhausen, 25 June anno 1708

The council at Mühlhausen released their organist with the condition that he would continue to supervise the organ renovation. Sebastian was happy to do this since he had a keen interest in the science of building organs. He also helped the council find a replacement. His cousin Johann Friedrich Bach came to Mühlhausen to take his place.

Sebastian and his wife left many friends in the little town that provided their first home. When the renovated organ was inaugurated the next year, they returned for the Reformation Festival. Sebastian performed a prelude he composed based on the melody *A Mighty Fortress is our God*. Over the years he would return again and again for performances of music he composed at the request of the town council.

Chapter Eight

Lord, I accept my calling and do what you have commanded, and will
in all my work surely do what You will have done; only help me…
~Passage of commentary on 2 Thessalonians 3:12 marked
by Johann Sebastian Bach in his *Calov Bible Commentary*

A Growing Family

Duke Wilhelm Ernst was a quiet and serious man. His motto was *Alles mit Gott* or *Everything with God*, and he promoted good church music. He founded an orphanage, restored the concept of confirmation and catechism to his churches, and built a new school staffed with distinguished teachers.

The castle chapel was called the *Way to the Heavenly City*. It was built into the east wing of the palace, and the important ceremonies were held there.

Sebastian admired the two tiers of galleries that ran along the walls. Ninety feet above his head, a rectangular opening was cut in the soaring ceiling for the music gallery. It was painted to look like the sky with clouds and angels. The musicians rested their music on the balustrade that lined the opening and performed for the congregation below them. Sebastian looked forward to playing heavenly music there.

* The Castle Chapel called the *Way to the Heavenly City*

The duke gave Sebastian a generous salary and arranged an apartment for the family in a house on the market square near his palace. Maria Barbara made their new home a welcoming place for musicians and friends.

Sebastian soon renewed his acquaintance with the royal family at the nearby Red Palace, who had employed him when he first left school. Duke Johann Ernst had recently died, and his older son Ernst August ruled as co-regent with his Uncle Wilhelm. He thought highly of Sebastian from the days when they played music together at his father's court.

The young duke played the violin and trumpet and still participated in the court performances. His younger brother, Prince Johann Ernst, was only ten years old, but he was already a violin virtuoso. He learned the keyboard and composition from Sebastian's cousin, Johann Gottfried Walther.

Sebastian was delighted to find his cousin there. They reminisced about their first meetings at Uncle Tobias's home. Cousin Gottfried was now organist at the church of St. Peter and St. Paul. The two cousins met often and liked to exchange four-part canons which they composed.

One evening Gottfried brought a new canon to show Sebastian, who sat at the clavichord and played the piece at once. "This is a brilliant piece," he said.

"It is quite impressive that you can play it at first glance," his cousin replied.

Sebastian returned to the music, running his fingers up and down the clavichord as he followed the written notes. "I believe I could play any composition at first sight."

Gottfried smiled but said nothing. The next day he invited his cousin for breakfast. While Gottfried prepared the food, Sebastian wandered over to the clavichord where a freshly-written composition stood tantalizingly on the music rack. He began playing the music in his confident style, when suddenly he stopped. He looked at the next passage and began again, but paused at the same place. He heard laughter behind him.

"Weren't you saying you could play any composition at first sight?" Gottfried said.

"No, the man does not exist who can play everything at first sight." Sebastian laughed—his cousin had proved him wrong.

Gottfried brought the toast to the table with a flourish. "Even Sebastian Bach has his limits."

The crowning joy of 1708 came at Christmas when Maria Barbara gave birth to their first child whom they named Catharina Dorothea. Her godmothers were Aunt Tobias's widow Catharina, and brother Christoph's wife Dorothea, who had been a second mother to Sebastian. She held a special place in Sebastian's heart, and perhaps for this reason, the little girl was always called Dorothea.

Pastor Eilmar from Mühlhausen was her godfather. Sebastian had grown fond of the pastor who championed sacred music in the church. In those days some churchmen shunned music as "worldly," but Pastor Eilmar insisted that the worship service should include music.

Sebastian rocked his new daughter in his arms as he softly sang an old Lutheran hymn. "We praise, we worship Thee, we trust. We give Thee thanks forever—O Father, that Thy rule is just, and wise and changes never."

On the last few lines Maria Barbara joined him. "Thy boundless power o'er all things reigns. 'Tis done whate'er Thy will ordains. Well for us that Thou rulest!" Sebastian gazed at his happy wife, who had given him this beautiful child. He felt that his cup of blessing was overflowing.

A knock on the door signaled the arrival of his apprentices. Martin Schubart was still with him, and his pupil from Arnstadt, Johann Caspar Vogler, was now old enough to leave home to become an apprentice. He was an eager student and rapidly learned Sebastian's method for the keyboard. Each day Sebastian oversaw his practice. He began with simple scales and then moved on to basic tunes that Sebastian wrote for him.

Today Martin brought fresh bread and soup, made by his landlady. "This is a gift in honor of the new baby," he said.

Maria Barbara took the food and the baby so that Sebastian could get to work, and soon the rhythmic sound of scales could be heard from the music room. The baby seemed to enjoy the sound and immediately fell asleep.

Sebastian worked throughout the morning with his apprentices. Martin was working on a complicated organ piece to play for one of the neighboring churches.

Sebastian listened to him play. Though he played with precision, there was something lacking. "When you play hymns, don't focus only on the melody," he told him. "Interpret the words as well."

He sat at the keyboard and played the hymn, fingering the keys slowly and softly for the passage about the death of Jesus, and then bursting into a joyous refrain as the words sang forth His triumph over sin. Suddenly Martin understood. He took his turn at the instrument and the music, which had been dull, came to life under his fingers. By the time they stopped to eat their bread and soup, Martin glowed with a new sense of power in his performance.

Johann, however, seemed discouraged after a difficult practice. "I will never master these simple tunes."

Sebastian spread his own fingers before the boy. "Look," he said. "You have the same number of fingers I have, and with much hard work you can play as I do."

Johann looked doubtfully at his own hands. They were smaller than his teacher's hands, and his fingers seemed much stubbier.

Sebastian laughed at his dubious expression. "Follow me! I will show you something in the organ loft."

With an air of mystery, Sebastian led him to the organ in the castle church and seated the boy next to him before the instrument. While Martin worked the bellows, Sebastian used his feet to play the pedals while his hands rested in his lap. With consternation Johann looked from his teacher's idle hands to the busy feet, while around him the music swelled in marvelous richness.

"You don't need your hands to play the organ," Sebastian said. "You just need to know how to move your feet." He laughed at his own joke.

Martin rested from the bellows work and grinned at Johann. "If Herr Bach can make music with just his feet, your stubby fingers should be able to play the clavichord."

One day Sebastian arrived home in a fancy uniform which the duke had given him.

"How dashing you look," exclaimed Maria Barbara.

Sebastian smiled ruefully. "The duke has decided to take the orchestra to perform in other courts."

"And well he should," Maria Barbara replied. "He has the finest orchestra in Germany."

"But how will you manage if I'm away for weeks at a time?"

His wife cradled baby Dorothea in her arms. "I'm fine at home."

"Would it help to invite your sister Friedelena to live with us?" he asked.

"A wonderful idea! Friedelena loves children, and she is like a mother to me."

Aunt Friedelena was delighted to join the family. She liked to say that she had things "at the ends of her fingers." If a stocking was lost, she had a replacement "at the ends of her fingers" or if the food was low in the pantry, she had a recipe "at the ends of her fingers" that only needed flour. Sebastian and Maria Barbara did not know how they had managed before she came. When Sebastian traveled, he knew the family was in good hands.

On one of these journeys he made the acquaintance of Georg Telemann who was concertmaster to Duke Johann Wilhelm of Saxe-Eisenach. Georg was still a young man, but had already composed numerous sacred works and instrumental music. In 1709 he loaned Sebastian his *Concerto in G Major for Two Violins* for him to make a copy.

* Georg Telemann

The two musicians shared an interest in combining national styles and genres of music. During one visit they experimented with a new composition. Georg played the clavichord and Sebastian the viola.

Georg turned from his instrument. "Have you tried the new form called the *cantata*?" he asked.

"I have done some early work with it," Sebastian said. "But I struggle with how to interpret the text into music."

Georg was thoughtful. "I try to interpret the text as a whole rather than elaborate on individual words."

Sebastian grinned as he remembered an opera he had heard in which the soloist went on for dozens of measures on a single word.

Georg leaned forward. "If you are serious about this art, I'd like to introduce you to Erdmann Neumeister who has written some of the best sacred poetry I have ever used in church music. He is visiting the court tomorrow."

"I've heard of him and would like very much to meet him."

Neumeister was fourteen years older than Sebastian and reminded him of his older brother Christoph. He spoke earnestly of the church liturgy and the importance of constructing worship around the word of God. He approved of Sebastian's desire to worship God through music. "I want you to make a composition with my librettos," he said.

Sebastian read the librettos that night. They were simple reflections on gospel themes, filled with the majesty and love of God. He returned home eager to begin composing.

On sunny afternoons Sebastian sat at his desk by the window and ruled smooth white pages with staves. As the music surged through his mind, he splashed the notes onto the page with a quill pen full of ink. Sometimes he vigorously scored out a section. Other times he jotted in blank corners or margins a new idea to use later. After years of study and effort, his powers of composition were maturing.

On November 22, 1710 Sebastian's first son was born.

They named him Wilhelm Friedemann, but they soon shortened his name to Friedemann. Sebastian's home was a busy place, with court musicians rehearsing, students practicing, and his own children in the midst. Little Dorothea liked to climb on the bench next to her father when he played the clavichord. She would listen with her eyes wide in wonder. Maria Barbara discovered that baby Friedemann liked best to sleep in the music room, so she tucked his cradle in the corner between the bass continuo and the clavichord.

As the years passed, more apprentices joined the family. In 1712 Philipp David Kräuter came to live with them for a year. He had a scholarship from the city of Augsburg to study with Sebastian. He was already an accomplished musician, so Sebastian made him an ambitious program of his own design.

"I want you to begin by studying this organ music by Frescobaldi who was one of the finest composers of the sixteenth century."

Philipp eyed the thick pile of music. "How many pages are there?"

"One hundred and four," said Sebastian with satisfaction. "This complex music fascinates me. I could not resist copying every page from the duke's music library."

The young apprentice looked doubtfully at the dense rows of notes. "Where do I begin?"

"Use these examples to put your brain to work rather

than your fingers. If you study them as I did, you will find the structure and musical ideas used to build the composition."

Philipp made rapid progress and soon reported back to his sponsors:

> "It is assuredly six hours per day of guidance that I am receiving, primarily in composition and on the keyboard, at times also on other instruments. The rest of the time I use by myself for practice and copying work, since he shares with me all the music I ask for. I am also at liberty to look through all of his pieces."

The next year the family of Duke Christian of Saxe-Weissenfels commissioned Sebastian to write a cantata for the duke's thirty-first birthday. Salomo Frank, a prolific hymn-writer who worked at the court with Sebastian, wrote a fantastical poem for the cantata which became known as the *Hunt Cantata*. Sebastian enjoyed composing for the large group of voices and instruments, including bassoons, violins, horns, oboes and recorders.

The cantata was a great success. "You handled the vocal forms in an exciting way!" declared one of the courtiers.

"The musical diversity is sublime," said his wife, fluttering her fan in her enthusiasm.

"Colorful and delicate textures," added the capellmeister, who came to congratulate Sebastian on his accomplishment. "I hope we'll have the opportunity to work together again."

The music was so enchanting that the duke increased Sebastian's salary, and the *Hunt Cantata* was performed again for Duke Ernst on his birthday.

The day after his return, Maria Barbara gave birth to twins, a boy and a girl. Georg Theodor Reineccius, the town choirmaster, was godfather to little Maria Sophia and Johann Christoph.

Sadly the little boy died soon after his birth, and his sister died three weeks later. Maria Barbara and Sebastian grieved the loss of their children. In his sadness Sebastian remembered what his mother had taught him about hope.

Though their children did not have the chance to live in this world, they had souls that would live forever. Holding Maria Barbara's hand, he tried to express this idea to her.

His words faltered, but an old hymn sprang to his mind. It began with praising Jesus, who was born to save us. As Sebastian softly sang, the flood of misery seemed to abate, and a feeling of hope returned. His little ones were in the care of One who left His heavenly throne to become a child.

> A little Child, Thou art our Guest
> That weary ones in Thee may rest;
> Forlorn and lowly is Thy birth
> That we may rise to heaven from earth.

Chapter Nine

The sole purpose of harmony is the Glory of God; all other use is but idle jingling of Satan.
~a quote from Gerhardt Niedt that Johann Sebastian Bach often quoted to his students

A Promotion

In the summer of 1713 the young Prince Johann Ernst returned from his grand tour of the Low Countries. He brought home so many manuscripts of music that he had to build more shelves in the Red Palace. There were French and German compositions and even Italian ensemble concertos. He shared his treasures with his teacher.

Sebastian was enchanted by the clear melodies. He copied many concertos by Vivaldi which were written for string and wind instruments. "I would like to arrange them for the clavier so that I can study the chain of ideas and their relation to each other," he told the prince.

As he studied the new compositions, he made a game of looking for the hidden harmonies. To entertain himself he would take a piece of music and create a new melody that harmonized with it.

He also experimented with using a variety of

modulations. He played one of his experimental pieces for Maria Barbara. "Listen and let me know if you can hear the melody progress from key to key."

She turned her lively eyes on him as he sat at the clavichord, and even little Dorothea stopped her play to listen to the music.

"It's enchanting," declared Maria Barbara. "So enchanting, that I did not perceive any change."

Sebastian smiled. "That was the effect I hoped for. If it is done correctly, every modulation introduces a new thought, but the audience hardly notices because it glides smoothly to the end of the piece."

At the time, the duke finished building his school, and he hired Sebastian's Ohrdruf schoolmaster, Herr Kiesewetter, to be the first headmaster. Sebastian welcomed his old friend, who had made his school a place of learning and culture. He invited him to the group that met at the Bach home to play music and talk. Herr Reineccius, who was choirmaster at the school, and Gottfried, Sebastian's cousin, also attended.

One day Herr Kiesewetter brought the new assistant headmaster to one of their evening meetings. His name was Johann Matthias Gesner, and he had a deep love for music.

Gesner became one of Sebastian's closest friends. Like Sebastian, he lost his father when he was young. He received a scholarship to attend school, and he distinguished himself in the study of languages.

*Johann Matthias Gesner

Watching Sebastian and Gottfried working a musical puzzle one day, he remarked, "Your game with fitting together bits of music reminds me of my old Greek teacher. He would test me by creating fragments of Greek so that I would have to reconstruct the text."

"That is an excellent idea for teaching students how to write music," Sebastian said. "Give them a melody and challenge them to construct a second melody that harmonizes with it. It will be like putting together the pieces of a lost masterpiece. I will try this with my apprentices."

Sebastian's group of apprentices continued to grow. In

the fall of 1713 Johan Lorenz Bach, the son of Sebastian's cousin, Valentin, arrived to serve as apprentice for the next five years.

Later Johann Tobias Krebs and Johann Gotthilf Ziegler joined him. The students used to make a pun about Krebs. Since his name meant "crab" and Bach meant "brook," they said that Krebs "was the only crab in the brook." Gotthilf Ziegler in particular showed promise in composition, and he become adept at Sebastian's game of composing from a single melody.

Increasingly churches asked Sebastian to examine their organs and give recitals. The audiences thrilled with delight at his clever improvisations. He played intricate music in a fresh and expressive manner.

In November1713 Sebastian was invited to Halle to consult on a massive organ renovation at the Church of our Lady. Halle was the hometown of George Frideric Handel, and his teacher had been the organist of this church.

The church needed an expert to supervise the expensive project. They asked Sebastian to audition for the post of organist. This organ would be built with sixty-three speaking stops and would be one of the grandest instruments in Europe.

Sebastian decided to audition. He remained for two weeks consulting on the renovation of the organ and preparing his audition piece. It was a cantata he composed for a text written by the pastor. The church board was so impressed by his performance that they immediately offered him the post. Sebastian thanked the board, but told them he would have to be released from his current position before he could accept their offer. He had much to think about as he returned home to Weimar.

The next month a special courier arrived at the court with a contract for Sebastian to sign in acceptance of the post. The duke insisted Sebastian wait until he discussed it with the co-regent, Duke Ernst.

At the same time, Sebastian worked feverishly to prepare the musical celebrations for the prince's seventeenth birthday and the Christmas season. Finally in January he made his formal request for dismissal. Duke Wilhelm's answer was firm. "You will have to tell the people of Halle that you cannot accept their call because you have been promoted to concertmaster in the court here…with a raise in salary."

The duke had just completed a two year renovation of the music gallery in the sanctuary. He expected to bring in a new era of music at court. His plan called for Sebastian to write a church cantata each month for the musicians of the orchestra.

Sebastian relished the opportunity to write new compositions. The first worship service after his promotion was an unusual day in the church calendar—both Palm Sunday and the Feast of Annunciation fell on that day.

For this important conjunction of holy days, Sebastian

wrote a cantata entitled *King of Heaven, Welcome,* based on Psalm 40:8-9: "I waited patiently for the LORD; and he inclined unto me, and heard my cry." In a clever twist on the idea of Jesus' triumphal entry into Jerusalem, the cantata ended with the anticipation of all believers entering the eternal Jerusalem.

He wrote the cantata for four voices, recorder, violin, two violas, violoncello, and organ. Martin Schubart played the organ, Sebastian took the lead violin, and his best students filled in as needed to augment the court capelle. Through the music, the humble instruments seemed transformed into voices expressing the joy of God. The words of the cantata spoke of faith and hope, of sin and forgiveness. The heavenly music filled the sanctuary, and Sebastian knew he had found his calling as a composer.

Sebastian enjoyed the experience of producing his works with the highly skilled court orchestra and vocalists. He often conducted the ensemble as he played the violin, the penetrating sound keeping the musicians in better order than direction from a harpsichord.

To the delight of the musicians, Sebastian tried a new idea of giving each of them a chance to play the solo lead.

"Next time write a piece for my cello," urged one musician. "The cello rarely gets to lead the orchestra."

"Don't forget the viola d'amore."

"Or the basso continuo."

"I will have to ask the duke to send me another ream of

paper if I am to accommodate all of you!" Sebastian said.

Though some composers wrote their music with only the framework, leaving the musician to add flourishes, Sebastian preferred to write every detail. Some of the movements were so fast that his musicians looked with misgivings at the scores before them. However, when they heard how the many parts came together, they saw the reason for his precision.

Often he wove two melodies rather than adding a bass harmony. He thought of it as two people talking with each other. One melody would speak for a time, and then the second melody would respond.

Sebastian was thankful for the salary that came with his promotion. Maria Barbara had just given birth to a son, whom they named Carl Philipp Emanuel. Though he had a long name, they soon settled for calling him Emanuel. Their household now contained three young children.

Georg Telemann, who lived in Frankfurt, traveled to Weimar to hold the baby at his baptism and stand as one of his godfathers. During his visit Georg told Sebastian about the loss of his wife three years before. "I went through such a valley of grief that I thought I would not survive. Then one day I was playing a hymn in church, and suddenly the Lord woke my soul to indescribable beauty and a great peace.

Sebastian remembered the sadness he felt after the loss of his twins. "There is a kind of miracle of healing that comes after a time," he said.

"For me it was THE miracle," replied Georg. "I have written about it and published a book called *Poetic Thoughts*."

"I wish Maria Barbara could read your book. At times we have been weighed down with sorrow."

Georg promised to send him a copy. The two musicians continued to correspond. Georg wrote glowing letters about his new position as music director in Frankfurt. He had the freedom to experiment with new types of composition. Sebastian considered the church cantatas Georg wrote to be the finest church music of his generation.

The duke was proud of Sebastian and often gave him permission to perform for other courts. Near the end of the year Sebastian played at the Court Church in Cassel before the German Prince Frederick I of Sweden. As he played the complicated piece, his feet flew over the pedals.

"It is like thunder in a storm!" exclaimed one of the courtiers.

The prince himself was so amazed that he took a valuable ring from his finger and gave it to Sebastian.

Chapter Ten

There shall no doubt deter me./ To thy word, Lord, I will hearken./ I believe that if thou depart,/ I can in this find comfort,/ That I, amongst the redeemed shall come to the welcome port.
~ translation of text used by Johann Sebastian Bach for his cantata *It is Good for You that I Depart*, 1725, BWV 108

The Champion of Germany

As the year 1715 began, Johann Bernhard Bach came to live with the family as an apprentice. He was the son of Sebastian's older brother Christoph. Sebastian could hardly believe that the little boy, whom he used to carry in his arms, was old enough to be an apprentice.

"I am not adept at studies, so Papa decided I should leave school to study music," he told his uncle.

"We will make you into a fine musician," Sebastian said. "It will be like the old days when I lived in your house, except now *you* are the cousin that all the little ones admire."

Dorothea, Friedemann and baby Emanuel adored their big cousin. He gave them piggy back rides along the cobbled streets outside their home and taught them to play the tin flute. They sat for hours listening to him practice on the harpsichord and clapped heartily at the end of every piece.

He also helped Dorothea with her schoolwork, since her mother was teaching her to read. He wrote out the words of hymns for her to practice and sing at the same time.

Sebastian enjoyed teaching his growing number of apprentices. As he worked with them to develop the skills they needed for the organ, he had the idea of writing preludes and fugues in every major and minor key. He laid out his plan in a leather-bound book that held 92 sheets. He planned to fill the book with music based on the classic hymns which he grew up singing in church. In time he called it the *Orgelbüchlein* which means *Little Book for the Organ,* and each of his students meticulously made their own copies. On the title page he wrote: *To God alone be given the praise for what is written here for man's use.*

Martin Schubart graduated from his apprenticeship and was now Sebastian's assistant. He helped the younger boys with their practice. He tried to pass on the lessons Sebastian had taught him, especially the idea of putting the proper feeling into the music. He knew that if he could help the students understand, the music would never be the same for them again.

Sebastian began work on new cantatas using hymns written by Salomo Franck. They had worked together before on the successful *Hunt Cantata.* The hymns expressed the love of God in a way that inspired Sebastian. For Easter that year, he composed a cantata that began "The heavens laugh! The earth doth ring with glory." The cantata ended with the dramatic chorale:

> So forth I'll go to Jesus Christ,
> My arm to him extending;
> To sleep I'll go and rest so fine,
> No man could ever wake me,
> For Jesus Christ, of God the Son,
> He will the heav'nly door unlock,
> To life eternal lead me.

In May of 1715 Johann Gottfried Bernhard was born. He was named for Sebastian's cousin, Johann Gottfried Walther, who was also his godfather. The family soon shortened his name to Bernhard. He was a chubby, healthy baby, and his big brothers and sister played tunes for him on the tin flute to make him laugh.

*Louis Marchand, (2 February 1669 – 17 February 1732)

When little Bernhard was still a toddler, the famous French musician Jean Louis Marchand visited the Saxon Court in Dresden. He had been a prodigy as a child, and his fame continued to follow him wherever he went. One day Sebastian arrived at rehearsal to find the musicians discussing Marchand.

"He was the organist of a cathedral at the age of fourteen," said Herr Eck, as he sat tuning his viola on his knee.

"I heard that he did not even have to apply for a post when he moved to Paris. They asked him which position he would like to fill," added Herr Ulrich, deftly replacing a reed in one of his wind instruments.

"Of course, he took the position as organist to the king," Herr Heininger said. He was a large, brawny man who played the trumpet when he was not performing his duties as palace steward.

Herr Hoffman gave a conspiratorial wink. He combined his talent of playing the violin with a gift for picking up gossip. "And then King Louis XIV exiled him for impertinence."

"Tell us," Herr Eck said.

"He was a bad husband, and when his wife left him, the king ordered him to give half his salary to her."

"What happened next?" Sebastian asked. Though he knew he should be starting rehearsal, he could not resist hearing the rest of the story.

"Marchand went to play the organ before the king and then suddenly stopped in the middle of the church service. He told the king that if his wife was to have half his salary, she could play half his music."

Herr Heininger whistled through his teeth. "No wonder the king exiled him."

Sebastian soon heard about Marchand again. Despite his brilliance, Marchand was so arrogant that the royal concertmaster wrote to Sebastian, begging him to come to Dresden to challenge the conceited musician to a contest. "Show him that Germany has great musicians too!" Herr Volumier wrote in his vigorous style.

Sebastian conferred with his fellow capelle musicians, and they told him that he must go. "The honor of Germany is at stake," Herr Eck said.

"And you are the only one who can rival Marchand on the keyboard," added Herr Heininger.

Sebastian traveled to Dresden the next week. Herr Volumier arranged for him to hear Marchand play. Sebastian listened with frank approval. "I have studied his music, and it will be a rare honor to make this challenge."

Sebastian wrote a letter of invitation to Marchand, proposing that he would perform *ex tempore* any musical task Marchand gave, with the expectation that Marchand would do the same. It was a daring idea, and Marchand accepted.

With his usual energy, Herr Volumier set up the contest and promoted it throughout the city. All over Dresden people talked of the anticipated concert.

On the evening of the contest Sebastian arrived at the home of Count Flemming. The house was filled with the most educated and fashionable people of Dresden, including Prince Ferdinand Augustus. He was the youngest brother of the crown prince Frederick, who would one day be known as Frederick the Great.

A trumpeter announced the arrival of Marchand. Sebastian turned to watch his entrance, but Marchand did not appear. The audience waited over an hour while a messenger was sent to his lodging. He returned with the story that the musician had left town. Apparently Marchand had heard Sebastian practicing in the music room earlier in the day. He was mortified to learn the quality of his opponent and promptly departed by express coach.

Though Marchand did not keep his part of the challenge, Sebastian sat at the harpsichord and began playing piece after piece of famous compositions. After this opening, he bowed to the king and asked him to sing out a melody for him to improvise. Prince Ferdinand Augustus bowed in his turn and sang a favorite tune. At once, Sebastian began improvising on the new theme. As the beautiful fugue blossomed under his skillful fingers, the admiration of the audience grew. The hush in the hall after his performance lasted a full minute before an uproar of applause shook the house. "Herr Bach!" shouted some of the younger men. "The champion of Germany!"

*Johann Sebastian Bach as a young man

Maria Barbara was delighted to hear of Sebastian's triumph. He told her about the glittering costumes of the royal courtiers and how the room was lit with so many candles that it seemed to be daylight.

"And I have been improving the time while I traveled by composing a cantata for one of Pastor Neumeister's poems. Let me sing it for you."

He sat at the clavichord and began singing the opening Bible verse: "Whoever loves me will keep my words, and my

Father will love him and we will come to him and make our dwelling with him."

Maria Barbara joined him for the choir's part, leaning lightly against him as she read the music over his shoulder:

O Lord, through the radiance of Your light
You have gathered to Your faith
People from all the languages of the world;
May this be sung, Lord, to Your praise.
Alleluia, alleluia.

As they finished, Maria Barbara sighed. "It's all very well to perform for the splendor of an earthly court, but this is music for the King of Kings."

Chapter Eleven

I had much distress in my heart, but your consolation restores my soul.
~translation of the text used by Johann Sebastian Bach in
cantata BWV 21

By the River of Babylon

Duke Wilhelm was quarreling with his nephew Duke Ernst, and he forbade his court to visit the Red Palace under penalty of a ten thaler fine. Since many of the musicians worked for both dukes, Sebastian did not pay attention to the order. His friendship with Duke Ernst was too great.

As a result Duke Wilhelm was angry with him and made a plan to punish him. At Weimar there was an elderly capellmeister named Herr Drese. Sebastian, as concertmaster, took care of most of Herr Drese's responsibilities because he was infirm. When the old capellmeister died, everyone assumed Sebastian would take his place. Duke Wilhelm, however, gave the post to Herr Drese's son.

Sebastian worried he would not be welcome in the court of Duke Wilhelm much longer. When he discussed his concerns with Duke Ernst, the duke had an idea that might solve the problem.

The previous year Duke Ernst had married the sister of Prince Leopold of Anhalt-Cöthen. When the prince heard Sebastian's performance at the wedding, he invited him to visit his home in Saxe-Weissenfels to conduct a performance of his *Hunt Cantata*.

Duke Ernst offered to write to the prince about the problem. Prince Leopold responded with enthusiasm. He was eager to employ the gifted concertmaster at his court.

On November 6, 1717 Sebastian asked to be dismissed from his post in order to serve as capellmeister for Prince Leopold. Duke Wihelm was shocked with the sudden request and refused to dismiss him. He was so angry that he placed him in jail for a month to make him change his mind.

Sebastian only grew more determined. He spent his time organizing and adding to his *Little Book for the Organ*. As the weeks passed, he completed forty-six pieces of music.

Finally on December second, as he was preparing to write his forty-seventh chorale, he was set free. The duke grudgingly discharged him. Martin Schubart, who had been his apprentice and assistant for so many years, remained in Weimar and replaced him as organist.

*****

Prince Leopold of Anhalt-Cöthen played the violin, the viol de gamba, and the clavier. He also sang a good bass. When Sebastian arrived for his first concert, the prince asked to play his violin with the musicians. Sebastian watched the prince performing, his eyes half-closed with the joy of the music, and he knew he would be happy at this court.

The prince provided living quarters for the family in a modest white-fronted house near the main gate of the castle. By Christmas the family was snug in their new home.

Prince Leopold did not require music for his chapel because he was a Calvinist and did not use elaborate music in the worship service. Sebastian was disappointed, but he threw himself into composing orchestral suites and cantatas for the court—almost one new work every week.

The prince paid a copyist to prepare the music for the orchestra. Over time he also paid to have the music bound, and the manuscripts soon covered several shelves. He was proud of the skill and artistry of his new capellmeister.

Sebastian was pleased to find the orchestra equipped with dozens of fine instruments and the court musicians of the highest caliber. They came from Berlin when the new Prussian king dissolved his father's court capelle.

Sebastian returned home to report to Maria Barbara after the first rehearsal. "It is a group of virtuosi like I have never seen. I have asked that we may have regular rehearsals at our house."

The townspeople grew accustomed to hearing the strains of melodic court music as the orchestra rehearsed each week. The cantor of St. Jacob's Church used the court musicians as an example to his choir. "Even the prince's musicians must rehearse and exercise faithfully if they would perform well," he said.

When spring came Aunt Friedelena took the children for walks across the bridge of the moat and past the sentries to the wide gardens around the castle. Dorothea was nine years old now and enthusiastically told her father about the view of trees and green pastures that surrounded the castle. Beyond the Elbe River the Harz Mountains rose majestically in the distance.

Friedemann, at seven years of age, would shout for joy when one of the prince's magnificent horses passed. Emanuel was three years old, and Bernhard was just learning to walk. They tumbled happily on the green turf that was once used for jousting.

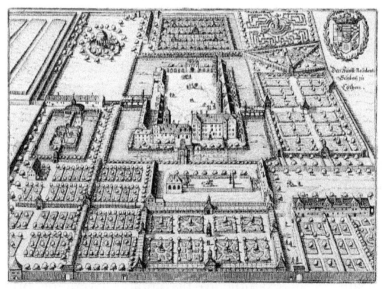

*Aerial view of Cöthen

The next year a baby boy was born to the Bach family, and Prince Leopold stood as his godfather. The child was named Leopold Augustus and was baptized in the castle chapel. To his parents' great sorrow, little Leopold Augustus died when he was only ten months old.

Maria Barbara and Sebastian grieved for their son. Once again Sebastian searched for a way to communicate hope to his wife. "We may feel that all is lost when they are taken from us, but this is not true," he told her. "The Lord was pleased to use us to bring a soul into the world, and the Lord has a plan for this child beyond our comprehension."

As Maria Barbara sobbed in his arms, he softly sang for her the last verse of an old hymn:

> We all confess the Holy Ghost,
> Who sweet grace and comfort giveth
> And with the Father and the Son
> In eternal glory liveth...
> All flesh shall rise, and we shall be
> In bliss with God eternally. Amen.

Every year Sebastian composed music for the prince's birthday in December and the celebration of the New Year. To celebrate New Year's Day in 1719, Sebastian composed a secular cantata using the writing of a popular poet named Christian Friedrich Hunold.

In the cantata, the voice of "Time" represented the past and spoke with a character called "Divine Providence" who represented the future. The prince praised the performance and often asked for sections to be performed again in the evening concerts.

Sebastian also composed several violin sonatas and some viola de gamba music for Prince Leopold since these were his favorite instruments. The prince spent hours every evening playing music with his orchestra, the music floating out over the towers and gabled roofs of the castle.

*Violin Sonata No. 1 in G minor from 1720 in Bach's handwriting

In 1719 news came that the great Handel would be visiting his hometown of Halle. Sebastian admired his compositions, especially the new *Water Music* which had been performed in London to wide acclaim. He traveled to

104

Halle to meet Handel, but to his disappointment, he missed him by a few hours.

Friedemann was nine-years old now. He had a handsome face and looked more like his mother than his father. Sebastian gave him simple exercises with both hands to teach him the keyboard. He made his son a notebook, and penned I.N.J. before the first finger exercise.

"These letters are the abbreviation for *In Nomine Jesu*. Do you remember what this means in Latin?"

"It means *In the Name of Jesus,*" Friedemann said.

Sebastian regarded his son solemnly. "I want you to understand that all your efforts, even a five-finger exercise, are in the name of the Lord and for His glory."

Sebastian began the notebook with an explanation of clefs and a guide to playing ornaments, which were half notes added to embellish the melody. Next he recorded traditional hymns, beginning with simple compositions. He also wrote the fingering for two pieces to show the best way to play the keyboard. He titled the book *Little Keyboard Book for Wilhelm Friedemann Bach.*

Sebastian had a theory about training children to be musicians. "Expose them to only the best music," he told Maria Barbara. "In this way they will become accustomed to what is excellent, and the right understanding will follow in time."

When Friedemann was ready to study the organ, his father wrote six sonatas for his lessons.

At their first lesson Sebastian sat at the organ and showed his son how to play the pedals. The glorious tones filled the sanctuary. "The pedal places the organ above all other instruments and gives it majesty," he said.

"Can I play the music you were playing just now, Papa?" Friedemann asked.

"Wait until you are ready," his father said. "You cannot fly before your wings are grown."

Friedemann worked hard at his exercises, especially his foot work. Sebastian was pleased to see that he had the makings of a gifted musician. "You are learning to use the pedal fully. If you keep working, you will learn how to give the pedal a part of its own."

When Prince Leopold traveled, he took his orchestra with him. He even had a special folding harpsichord made for traveling. In July 1720, Sebastian accompanied him to Carlsbad, where the prince's physician recommended the waters for his health.

While he was away, tragedy struck. Sebastian returned home to discover that his beloved Maria Barbara had died suddenly. Aunt Friedelena met him at the door. Her face was gray, and she seemed to have shrunk upon herself.

"Sebastian, I must bring you sad news," she said. She wanted to tell him before he saw the children. The shock had barely hit him when the children ran in and clung to him. "But I don't understand," he said numbly. "She was healthy when I left."

Aunt Friedelena was crying now. "It was something sudden. There was nothing the doctor could do."

Emanuel was only six, but he hugged his father and whispered, "The full choir from Wilhelm's school sang at her funeral, Papa."

Sebastian felt lost without his Maria Barbara to anchor their family. For the next few months he followed his routine in a kind of stupor. Every day he ate his breakfast with the family, instructed his apprentices and quietly rehearsed the orchestra. After the midday meal the prince would hold an interview with him to plan the next evening performance. Sebastian tried to show enthusiasm for the program, but inside he felt empty.

Only in the loneliness of the chapel could he find true peace. Every afternoon he sat at the organ and let the music billow out his sadness and fill the empty spaces with calm. One day he played the hymn he used to sing with Maria Barbara: "We praise, we worship Thee, we trust. We give Thee thanks forever—O Father, that Thy rule is just, and wise and changes never."

The aching sorrow for his wife suddenly burst from him, and he wept as he had not been able to weep in the first days following her death. When the grief had spent itself, he returned to the hymn and played it through again. In his heavy sorrow, his hope in his heavenly Father was his comfort.

Four months after his wife's death Sebastian visited

Hamburg to perform in several recitals and to consider taking a post there. In the audience were many outstanding musicians including the famous organist Adam Reinken.

Reinken was ninety-seven years old now, but Sebastian remembered walking many miles to hear him play when he was still a choirboy. As Sebastian played the exquisite four-manual organ, he poured out his heart through the music. He played an improvisation on *An Wasserflüssen Babylon* as a tribute to Reinken who had written a famous work with this title.

The theme was based on Psalm 137, and the sadness of the words welled up in his heart: "By the river of Babylon we sat down and wept when we remembered Zion." The last remnants of grief over his wife's death seemed to heal as he played the music: "How shall we sing the Lord's song in a strange land?" He was not alone in his suffering, and his Lord would help him through the strange path he must walk without his Maria Barbara.

For over two hours the music flowed from him. The aged Reinken sat in solemn joy listening to the music. "I thought this art was dead," he said to Sebastian. "But I see it still lives in you."

The months passed and Sebastian and his children grew accustomed to the routine of a home without Maria Barbara. Aunt Friedelena did what she could to make the home a comfortable place, and slowly the sadness melted.

Chapter Twelve

"It pleased God that I should be called hither to be Director Musices and Cantor at the St. Thomas School."
~letter by Johann Sebastian Bach to his friend, George Erdmann in 1730

Music Director

As the snows of 1721 melted, Sebastian composed six concertos which he presented to the Margrave of Brandenburg for his birthday. He was one of the princes of the Prussian royalty and a devoted patron of the arts. Sebastian also performed the Brandenburg Concertos in Cöthen for Prince Leopold, who admired the use of the new type of horns which were just coming into vogue.

One evening the prince told Sebastian that a gifted soprano would be performing at his court. She was the daughter of a court trumpeter and had been carefully trained by her father. When Sebastian heard her trilling voice, he was entranced. Her name was Anna Magdalena Wilcken, and she became court soprano at the castle in Cöthen.

Working with Anna Magdalena each week at rehearsals and performances, Sebastian grew to admire her kind nature and cheerful disposition. She also attended the same church, and he had many opportunities to make her acquaintance. Soon she was coming home with him after the worship service to visit the children.

Aunt Friedelena noticed the growing affection between them and encouraged Sebastian to ask her to be his wife. "An aunt is all fine and good, but children need a mother," she told him. A year and a half after the loss of his first wife, Sebastian married Anna Magdalena on December 3, 1721. The Bach home was filled with music and laughter once again.

A week after their marriage, the prince married as well. Sebastian played an important role in the five weeks of festivities following the wedding, and Anna Magdalena sang in the concerts. Sebastian even wrote an ode for the event.

When the excitement of the royal wedding died down, Sebastian created a notebook for his new wife and used it to teach her the keyboard. Each week he wrote some music in it. Sometimes he composed a piece, and other times he copied music by other composers. He also recorded a wedding song he wrote for her:

> Your servant, sweetest maiden Bride:
> Joy be with you this morning!
> To see you in your flowery crown
> And wedding-day adorning
> Would fill with joy the sternest soul.
> What wonder, as I meet you,
> That my fond heart and loving lips
> O'erflow with song to greet you?

*Title page of the Clavier Buchlein for Anna Magdalena Bach

Anna Magdalena grew especially close to Dorothea whom she taught to sing. Her new daughter had a clear soprano voice, and the two sang duets while Sebastian played the clavichord.

He had a high regard for the many musical talents of his wife. She continued to work as a court vocalist until their first child was born. She also helped Sebastian copy music for his orchestra. She had a neat music hand which became so similar to her husband's handwriting that few could tell the difference.

Many evenings after the children said their prayers and went to bed, Sebastian and Anna Magdalena transcribed music together until late at night.

In 1722 Sebastian received his own seal. It was created using the letters J.S.B. combined with their mirror image to create the design. He used it throughout the rest of his career.

*The seal of Johann Sebastian Bach

In the fall of 1722 Sebastian's friend Georg Telemann stopped by on his way home from Leipzig. The city council was looking for a music director for the St. Thomas School, and his friend urged Sebastian to apply. "It is a prestigious position because the music director is responsible for the music of the four main churches in Leipzig. He has the town musicians for the church services as well as the school choir. It would give you marvelous scope for composing sacred works."

"Why don't you apply yourself?" Sebastian asked.

Georg looked embarrassed for a moment. "I have applied, but after consulting with my own city council, I prefer to stay in Hamburg."

"I have visited Leipzig many times," Sebastian said. "It has a tradition of fine music."

"And your sons could attend the university there."

Over the next few weeks Sebastian continued to ponder his friend's advice. He did not know what to do, but Anna

Magdalena had a solution. "Go to the prince and ask him what he would advise. The politics are changing, and he will know what is best."

As a result, on a blustery February morning Sebastian sought the prince in his study. When he explained his dilemma, the prince smiled sadly. "I will miss you, dear friend, but I believe this post could be for the best. As you know, my resources have decreased, and my wife suggests that I spend less on my court musicians and other musical hobbies." He sighed, and Sebastian noticed that the prince appeared more tired than usual. "I want you to know that I will keep you as honorary capellmeister of my court and will always welcome you and your wife as guest performers."

When the time came for Sebastian's audition, Prince Leopold prepared a letter of recommendation. He wrote that "we have at all times been well content with his discharge of his duties," and assured the council that he gave his approval to Sebastian's request for dismissal, adding: "We give him highest recommendation for service elsewhere."

At the audition Sebastian performed two church cantatas that he composed for the occasion. For the performance he worked with the town musicians. He found them a well-trained group. There were eight salaried members, and they all played multiple instruments. Gottfried Reicha directed this talented ensemble and had become a legend in Germany for his incredible flair with both wind and string instruments. In addition, apprentices increased the orchestra to twenty musicians.

The council questioned Sebastian about his ability to teach. Usually choir directors also taught Latin and catechism. They permitted him to hire an instructor to teach these subjects, but he would be required to instruct the boys' choir and private lessons for orchestral instruments. His years of experience with his apprentices also helped his application. He brought some of the workbooks he had created for his students to demonstrate his teaching style.

The city council voted in favor of Sebastian. "We need a famous man," the burgomaster said. "A famous man will make Leipzig renowned and will inspire the university students to participate in church music."

*Leipzig

The winter snows had melted and the fields were green with new grass when the Leipzig Council sent two carriages to bring the Bach family to their new home. Sebastian rode in the carriage with the boys. Friedemann was twelve now, and Emanuel was nine. Bernhard told the coachman that he was almost eight and must ride with "the men."

Anna Magdalena rode in the second carriage with Dorothea, Aunt Friedelena and the new baby, who was named Christiana Sophia Henrietta. Dorothea, at fourteen years of age, held her new sister at every opportunity, and the baby now slept in her arms.

The carriages creaked over the plains through rich pastureland and dense pine forests. Gradually the landscape changed to meadowland, with a sluggish river winding in the distance. The children watched from the windows, calling out when they spotted oxen pulling carts or water wheels churning at a mill house.

Suddenly Bernhard gave a shout. "See the walls, Papa! And the grand towers!"

"It is the city of Leipzig, little one," Sebastian replied.

The coachman hurried up the horses, and soon the family rode through the lush gardens surrounding the city walls. Lime trees lined the road, and a great stone gate opened onto the wide avenue of Leipzig.

Friedemann and Emanuel twisted in their seats, first pointing to the ancient tower that guarded the city, then admiring the fanciful signs on every side. A ferocious bear reared on his hind legs on the Black Bear Tavern sign, while white swans swam on a blue lake on the sign of the Three Swans Inn. The town houses towered four stories high. They had steep roofs with dormer windows jutting out along the top. The grander homes had carved timbers and golden decorations.

Sebastian caught sight of the cupola and sloped roof of the St. Thomas Church, and then the carriages glided through the gates and into an open square. They stopped next to a stone fountain in the middle of the courtyard. To one side was the long white building of the St. Thomas School, and at a right angle sat the vast bulk of the church.

The children, still in awe of their new surroundings, filed out of the coach, and received a warm greeting from the headmaster. His name was Herr Ernesti, and he invited them to come through a door on the far side of the school, which opened into their own apartments.

The children eagerly peeked into the two ground floor rooms and skipped down the four steps at the back of the hallway. "It's a wash house and cellar," Dorothea said with authority, when the boys asked about the tiny rooms.

Emanuel bolted back to the hallway and up the main staircase to the second level. He found the dining room and two bedrooms which looked onto the church square. "See how small our carriages look from here," he said.

On the opposite side of the apartment, Dorothea found the parlor and a small study next to it. "Boys, come see the

116

view from this window! We can see outside the town wall, and there's a river and a meadow."

Friedemann tried a door from the hallway next to the study and found a room lined with shelves full of manuscripts. "This is the school's music library," Herr Ernesti explained, puffing to keep up with the boys. "And the door there leads to the auditorium for the *secunda* class."

He opened the door for them, and they clustered around to look inside. "We use this classroom for teaching and rehearsal," he said.

Sebastian had come up behind them and nodded with approval.

"We have space for one hundred and fifty day pupils and dormitories for sixty choral scholars," Herr Ernesti said proudly. "And now I must leave you." He gave a quick bow and disappeared through the door at the other end of the classroom.

The boys returned to their apartment and found another stairway leading to three more rooms on the third floor. They claimed the largest of these for their bedroom. Their father called up to them to stop racing around, and they came downstairs to help unpack the cart.

The drivers carried the heavy furniture up the stairs, and Anna Magdalena directed where everything should go. Dorothea unpacked the pots and pans, and the kitchen sparkled with freshly polished copper and brass. Aunt Friedelena hummed while she set the silver candlesticks on the mantle, and Anna Magdalena polished the coffee pot and sugar basin for the table. "We are ready for guests," she said merrily.

As the last items were put away, Sebastian hung the picture of his father in its golden frame above the mantle, and next to it the delicate painting of Anna Magdalena. They had arrived in their new home.

On the thirtieth of May, 1723 Sebastian took his place in front of the choir of the St. Nicholas Church. He looked up to the organ loft and the gallery where the orchestra awaited his cue. Slowly he raised his hands to begin, and the music swelled around him like a powerful wind, carrying the choir's words up to heaven.

For this first Sunday directing the church music, Sebastian had composed a cantata to explain the gospel reading, which told the story of the Rich Man and Lazarus. He began the cantata with a verse from the twenty-second Psalm: "The meek shall eat and be satisfied: those who seek Him shall praise the Lord! May your hearts live forever." Sebastian designed part of the cantata to be sung after the sermon.

It concluded with a stanza from the well-known poem: *What God does—is done well:*

> What God does—is done well.
> I shall cling to this thought.
> On the rough road
> I may be driven by distress, death and misery,

Yet God will, like a father,
Hold me in His arms.
Therefore I let Him alone rule over me.

As the final notes faded on the air, Sebastian knew he had found a purpose here in Leipzig. From his earliest days as a church organist, he dreamed of church music that would combine the full scope of Bible truth with artistic ability. His new position would give him this opportunity.

For weeks after the first cantata, the people of Leipzig talked of nothing but the marvelous works of the new music director. For each Sunday and holy day, he composed a new cantata. He saw it as his greatest undertaking, and the Leipzig council marveled at his creativity. It was a promising start for Sebastian.

*The St. Nicholas Church, 18th century

Chapter Thirteen

Thirsting, Lord, for thee!/ Thine I am, O spotless Lamb;/ I will suffer nought to hide thee,/ Nothing else I ask beside thee.
~ translation of hymn text by Johann Franck used by Johann Sebastian Bach in his motet *Jesus, my Joy* 1723, BWV 227

Christmas Caroling

Snowflakes whirled around the dome of the St. Thomas Church as Sebastian prepared the choir for the Christmas cantata. The full orchestra was in attendance, tightening bowstrings and tuning instruments. Some of the smaller boys were fidgeting, but everyone grew quiet as he opened the rehearsal in prayer.

Before he began he made a sweeping motion with his arm to take in the full choir and all the instrumentalists. "In our music we want to reflect the personality and spirit of the work of Jesus on earth," he told them. "It is worth every effort we can give."

The rehearsal began, and Sebastian listened to all the parts at once, marking time with one arm. He sometimes nodded or raised a warning finger with his other hand when an instrument or choir section went astray.

In a surprisingly short time the choir and musicians became a unified group. "My soul magnifies the Lord, and my spirit rejoices in God, my Savior," the choir sang in Latin. The ancient words echoed in the sanctuary, giving Sebastian a momentary vision of Christians through the ages singing these same words.

The next week the school boys gathered for Christmas caroling. Friedemann and Emanuel, dressed in their black school uniforms and cloaks, waited impatiently while Dorothea smoothed their hair and made sure they had their song books. She looked them over one last time. "You will be a credit to Papa," she declared.

At her word, the boys dashed through the door to the school music room where the singers were already collecting. The prefects looked harassed as they tried to gather their groups around them. "Chorus primus, here!" Prefect Weiss shouted.

"Chorus secundus here!" Prefect Braun called.

Friedemann nudged Emanuel, who seemed dazed by the noise, and pointed him toward his group. "I'll see you back at school."

Heavy flakes of snow fell on Sebastian's dark cloak, as he waited at the door to send off each group. "Go forth to celebrate the birth of our Savior," he said.

Sebastian led the last group, the chorus primus, down the streets to the Market Square. They took up their first stand in front of the Apel House, the royal residence in

Leipzig.

At the first note of song, the lights came up in the second floor windows and bewigged heads looked down on the choir.

"Glory to God in highest Heaven," the choir sang in four part harmony. The snow swirled gently around them, and the music transformed the Market Square to a humble stable in Bethlehem long ago.

Thomaskirchhof, Burgstrasse, Thomasgassgen—street after street the student choir walked through the snow and stopped to sing at the houses decorated for Christmas. Many householders gave them treats like gingerbread and warm cider, and all of them gave a donation to the school.

At last they made their final procession past the night watchman calling the hour of nine o'clock. They arrived home weary but filled with the wonder of Christmas.

The year began, and Sebastian's ambitious plan to compose a cantata each week meant that every month he worked with the pastors to select the texts for a block of time, usually six weeks. He arranged them in booklet form and sent the drafts for publication in advance. His students and children later delivered the booklets to subscribers.

Every Monday he began with a stack of fresh paper and lined the sheets for his composition. Remembering his early Latin lessons in school, he wrote J.J. at the beginning of his scores. J.J. were the initials for *Jesu Juva* or *Jesus, help me*.

As he composed the choruses, arias, recitatives and

chorales for the week, he recorded the more complicated pieces first to allow time for copies to be made for the soloists and orchestra. At the end he wrote S.D.G. for *Soli Deo Gloria (To God Alone the Glory)*.

Several older students helped copy the performance parts while Sebastian proofed them for accuracy. Meanwhile he rehearsed small groups of instrumentalists and finally conducted one complete rehearsal on Saturday. On Sunday he conducted the cantata for two worship services. Monday morning he began the process again.

One of his supreme joys was teaching the students to sing and play instruments for the church orchestra. Waving the student handbook, he told the students: "The school regulations say that our part in worship is a good deed which the heavenly host pursues with greatest pleasure. We must take this duty seriously!"

Sebastian used the best singers to form the choir which performed the Sunday cantata. They sang for the two largest churches which were St. Nicholas Church and St. Thomas Church. The students performed in the morning at one church and the afternoon at the other, on an alternating schedule.

Sebastian assigned the students who were musically gifted, but not yet fully trained, to the *chorus secundus*. They sang at the alternating church service without the cantata. The *chorus tertius* contained students with less ability, and they sang at St. Peter's Church. His beginners' choir sang at the

New Church.

Sebastian worked hard, starting each day before the sun rose and working late into the night. He taught the choirs and met with smaller groups to rehearse for church services. He supervised week-day services at four churches, in addition to the hospital and the prison.

Once a month, Sebastian served as "inspector" of the school for a week. This meant conducting the morning and evening prayers with the students and saying the prayer before and after each meal. He also supervised the reading of the Bible or a history book during the meal. When the students were away from school for a funeral or performance, he would check them in. Each day he visited the students in the infirmary.

Outside of school hours the house stirred with activity with students practicing their instruments, Anna Magdalena directing the household, and the littlest children always in the midst. Sebastian would sit at his desk, surrounded with stacks of paper, ink pots, quills and rulers, composing music while one of his young children sat on his lap. "I'm like the viola in the chamber orchestra—I like to be in the middle of the harmony," he would say.

Sebastian also directed the student choir as it performed at weddings and funerals. At first they sang motets by other composers. Soon he began writing his own motets so the students could practice singing in parts.

One of the favorite motets for funerals became *Jesus, my*

Joy. The students sang repetitions of phrases so that the meaning seemed to come in waves: "There is therefore now no condemnation for those who are in Christ Jesus."

In the final section they sang: "For those who love God, their afflictions must also be pure delight. No doubt, here I suffer mockery and scorn, yet you also endure suffering, Jesus, my joy." The funerals were a solemn time for Sebastian, who felt closer to God as the choir sang about hope in the Lord.

As he continued to teach students on the organ, he realized they needed the opportunity to play in church. He wrote instrumental solos for them to perform during the communion service, designing the music to help the students improve their technique.

In addition to directing the choir, Sebastian occasionally taught Latin and catechism when the paid instructor could not teach. One week Sebastian taught the catechism class. The students recited their lessons, but they seemed bored.

"Lessons and music—they are like life! You must repeat and practice again and again to really learn," he said.

One of the small boys raised a hand. "But Herr Bach, it is hard to learn so much all at once."

"You learn your choir songs every week, don't you?" he asked.

"But music is easier to learn," the boy said.

At home Sebastian thought about the class and decided to compose some motets to teach Bible lessons the boys could understand. The next day he had his composition ready for the class.

The students sang in German: "Sing unto the Lord a new song" and "Praise the Lord for His mighty acts!/ Let everything that has breath praise the Lord." He let them practice this part several times, hoping the meaning would grow stronger.

Next he taught the chorale stanza. He sat and listened reverently as the choir of young voices swelled into song: "As a father has mercy/for all his children/ the Lord will also forgive us/ when we as children purely fear Him." He prayed that his students would keep this lesson with them always. This experience soon led to another project of arranging the catechism hymns of Martin Luther for the students.

Perhaps it was the respect the boys had for Herr Bach's musical expertise, or perhaps it was the Bible lessons, but discipline problems which had plagued the choir in the past disappeared when Sebastian directed the choir.

Chapter Fourteen

He came new life and hope to give/ That henceforth man to Him should live,/ To perfect freedom rising./ And shall the Son of God sustain/ The weight of all our guilt in vain,/ Mankind his Cross despising?
~ translation of text used by Johann Sebastian Bach for the closing chorale of Part I of the *St. Matthew Passion*

Picander

Sebastian's son Friedemann was thirteen years old now and showed great promise as a musician. Sebastian began teaching him composition. One evening they worked together in Friedemann's attic room. As the wind whistled under the roof tiles, Sebastian carefully ruled a white page with musical staves. "Composition is like writing a story," he explained. "Each musical part is a person, and they are making a great conversation. Pay attention to each part and don't let it end until it has finished what it has to say."

For this lesson he wrote the bass line from a hymn. Remembering the idea of fragments that Herr Gesner had shared with him, he instructed his son to write a tenor and alto part, each on a different stave. "In this way you will separate the parts and be able to see the harmonic progression accurately."

Friedemann bent over the page and slowly wrote the notes for the tenor line. The first line seemed easy, but when he tried to write the second line he got confused.

His father nodded in understanding. "Let me show you an example." He brought out a composition by Georg Telemann and rapidly copied the individual harmonies onto a fresh piece of paper. "Do you see how each line has its own part?" he asked.

Friedemann slowly ran his finger along the lines. "I can see it. Let me try again."

Though Friedemann was a good student, he rarely exerted himself to excel at school work. In the study of composition, however, he eagerly followed the lessons his father set him and worked hard to write his own beginning compositions.

When Sebastian had musicians visiting for dinner, Friedemann would linger at the table and listen to the men talking about music. One evening Georg Telemann stopped by for dinner as he traveled on his way to Hamburg. He finished the last bite of his apple cake, and sat back with a sigh. "Friedemann my boy, I hear you have taken to scribbling music like your father."

"Papa is teaching me," Friedemann said. "But I'm finding it hard to write something original."

"Listen to the best music you can. With time your experience will guide you to good judgment," said the old composer.

"But I have ideas that seem to lead nowhere."

Telemann smiled. "It's a common problem for the beginner. You must begin by looking for consistency of expression, *then* you can add variety of style."

Friedemann listened to his advice, and soon he was writing music that met with his father's approval. It was a great day when his father had him copy one of his compositions into his mother's music notebook.

On February 26, 1724 a son was born to Sebastian and Anna Magdalena. They named him Gottfried Heinrich. Sebastian held his newborn son while he worked energetically on a new cantata based on the gospel of John. As he studied the book of John, he was moved by the powerful story of Jesus becoming the victor by his death on the cross.

For Good Friday, Sebastian conducted the *St. John Passion* for the first time. The congregation found the words inspiring, but also surprising, as when the chorus sang, "If Thou didst not choose a slave to be,/ We all would be slaves eternally."

Students began to come to the Leipzig University in order to combine their education with the study of music under Johann Sebastian Bach. One such student was named Heinrich Nikolaus Gerber. He was so shy that he could not find the courage to meet the famous musician during his first six months in Leipzig.

At last, a friend introduced Heinrich. Sebastian greeted

him warmly as a fellow-countryman, since he was a native of Schwarzburg. When he learned that Heinrich hoped to study music, he made space in his schedule to teach the young man.

He gave him his *Inventions* for the first lesson. Next he assigned him a series of suites and the works he was assembling as *The Well-tempered Clavier.* When the young man hesitated over how to play the music, Sebastian played it through for him three times.

"It was the happiest hour of my life," Heinrich told his friends at the university. He proved to be a dedicated student. In two years he mastered a great amount of material and later became a distinguished composer and court organist.

One day a dapper young man presented himself at the door of the Bach home. He seemed barely older than Friedemann, but he wore the clothes of a civil servant. "Please tell your father that Christian Friedrich Henrici would like to meet him," he told Dorothea when she opened the door.

Sebastian asked him into his study and offered him a chair. "Are you looking for a teacher in music?" he asked kindly.

The young man laughed as though this were a clever joke. "I'm afraid I'm not musical at all. I'm a lawyer here in Leipzig, but I also write poetry. You may have seen my work under the name of Picander."

Sebastian recognized the name. "You sent me one of your poems and asked if I might put it to music. I'm sorry that I did not recognize you, but I expected a much older man."

"Old or young, do you like my poem?"

"I have already composed the music for it. Would you like to hear it?"

Herr Henrici listened with delight as Sebastian played his composition and Anna Magdalena sang the words.

"It's marvelous," he said, his voice choked with emotion. "I did not know that words could have such power."

Sebastian took his wife's hand. "Your poetry certainly sounds lovely when my wife sings it. We hope you will write many more poems for us. In fact I have an idea that we could use them for our church service."

Soon Herr Henrici was a frequent guest at the Bach home. He liked to hear the progress that Sebastian made on setting his poetry to music. On Sundays he sat in church and listened with profound pleasure to the cantatas Sebastian had composed for his words. "Such power," he would mutter to himself.

One evening Herr Henrici invited Sebastian to attend a gathering at a fashionable home. A footman opened the door on a crowded room glittering with the reflection of light from silver and glass.

"I want you to meet our hostess," said Herr Henrici. "This is Marianne von Ziegler. She has kindly offered her home as a salon for writers and musicians in Leipzig."

Sebastian bowed and looked into the lively eyes of Frau von Ziegler.

"I have enjoyed your performance on the organ at St. Thomas Church," she said. "Your playing is truly wonderful."

"There is nothing wonderful about it," replied Sebastian. "You merely strike the right note at the right moment and the organ does the rest."

Frau von Ziegler laughed. "My husband was an officer, and he used to say the same about the cavalry: you face in the right direction and your horse does the rest."

Herr Henrici held a small book of poetry. "And I suppose you would say when you write, you simply dip your pen in the ink and the pen does the rest?"

"There is some truth in that," replied Frau von Ziegler.

"All the same, I think Herr Bach would like to see these devotional poems. He might find some good material for his cantatas."

Sebastian took the book and read the opening verse of one of the sacred poems: "Come, come, my heart is open to You. Ah, let it be Your dwelling place!" After reading a few lines he realized he was holding a treasure trove of material. "May I have your permission to set your poetry to music for the church, Frau von Ziegler?"

His hostess was delighted. Sebastian used her verses for nine consecutive Sundays and festivals around Easter. The congregation admired the poignant words which added a personal touch to the devotional music.

*Christiana Mariana von Ziegler

In April 1725 Christian Gottlieb was born to the family. Anna Magdalena held their newest son while Sebastian softly played a lullaby on the clavichord. At this time the final page of the music book that Sebastian made for Anna Magdalena was filled, and he began a second book for her. He found that music was one way he could express his love for her.

He continued to copy compositions in this book throughout his life. The next year he wrote some special music in her book to celebrate the birth of another daughter. They named her Elisabeth Juliana Frederica, and she became known as Lieschen.

A few months later tragedy struck when their three-year-old daughter Christiana died. Sebastian and Anna Magdalena grieved for their precious child who was taken from them so young.

In the sadness of losing Christiana, Sebastian began composing a cantata from the gospel of St. Matthew. He wrote it on an epic scale and included more instruments and voices than he had ever used before: three choirs and two orchestras. The theme was the death of Christ, and he poured his own anguish into the composition.

The cantata had a part called the *application*. Sebastian composed it to be sung in a bass aria: "Gladly, whatever the cost, I welcome the cross and cup, in the same manner as it was offered the Savior to drink."

Sebastian discovered that the letters BACH created a melody, since the letter B was used in musical notation for B flat and the letter H was used for B natural. On the phrase "I welcome the cross and cup" he used the inverted melody of his own name as a way to claim this truth for his own. In his love for his Savior, he would welcome the cross and cup whatever the cost, even when the suffering of this world almost overwhelmed him.

Sebastian conducted the *St. Matthew Passion* for Good Friday. His masterpiece, which he began at one of his moments of great suffering, drew from an amazing variety of forms used in sacred and secular music. The poetry was written by his young friend Herr Henrici, and it had a lyrical quality that stirred the emotions. He also wove in verses from the Bible.

The congregation listened as the dialogue opened with "See him! How? Just as a lamb!" The response reverberated from the chancel side of the church: "O innocent lamb of God."

The cantata pictured the multitude of believers ascending to Mount Zion with music that sounded like a funeral march. The daughters of Zion called on the faithful to join them in witnessing the death of Christ.

As the last notes of music died among the arches of the sanctuary, the heaviness of the death of the Savior of the world settled on the congregation. They would have to wait until the triumphant fanfare of trumpets opening the cantata on Easter Sunday to celebrate the rest of the gospel: death was overcome in Jesus Christ!

Herr Henrici was so moved by the cantata that he remained in the sanctuary long after the worship service. "Surely, this is one of the most glorious expressions of the sacrifice of our Savior that the world has ever heard," he said.

Chapter Fifteen

We have one God of salvation and one Lord, who rescues us from death.
~The text based on Psalm 68:21 set into the funeral music for Prince Leopold by Johann Sebastian Bach

The Collegium Musicum

On a raw evening in February, three men sat by the fire in Sebastian's home. Sebastian was holding out a woodwind instrument for his friends to see.

Herr Eichentopf took up the instrument and blew gently into the mouthpiece. "A nice sound. May I take this back to my workshop to study?"

Sebastian laughed. "That's why I brought it back for you. I hoped you could make us a few more for the choir ensemble."

The third man lit his pipe and leaned back in his chair. He was Herr Hoffmann, who built and maintained the St. Thomas School instruments. "I was sure you brought us here to reveal some new innovation in the clavichord. You've been speaking mysteriously all week."

Sebastian patted a bulky shape by his chair. It was

covered with a brown velvet cloth, and Herr Hoffmann had been stealing glances at it during their meal.

"Come, come, you have left us in suspense long enough," Herr Eichentopf said.

"This is the first of its kind in Leipzig," Sebastian said.

Herr Hoffmann leaned forward. "Is it from your friend, Silbermann, the famous organ builder?"

"Yes, when he was here to stand as godfather to my son, he asked my opinion on his first model."

"Ha!" said Herr Eichentopf. "I'm sure you found something to improve."

Sebastian was not embarrassed by this comment. The three friends were always trying to help each other find excellence in their music. "As a matter of fact, it was too hard to play and the high notes were too weak."

"I imagine your friend was disappointed by your opinion," Herr Hoffmann said.

"It was hard at first, but he soon agreed with me. Now he has an instrument that is extraordinary." Sebastian twitched at the velvet covering which fell in a heap to reveal an exquisite keyboard instrument in a wooden case. "It is called a *hammerklavier*."

Herr Hoffmann forgot his pipe in his eagerness to inspect the instrument. "Can you play it for us?"

Sebastian sat at the keyboard and began playing one of his concertos.

"Remarkable," exclaimed Herr Eichentopf.

Herr Hermann wanted to inspect the key action, and they spent a pleasant evening examining and testing the instrument.

Herr Eichentopf was the last to have a turn playing the keyboard. He chuckled with delight as the silvery tones rolled under his fingers. "Sebastian, if you want to promote this hammerklavier, you must publish compositions that use it."

The idea intrigued Sebastian. "I have a book of exercises I've been developing for the keyboard. Perhaps I should publish them."

Herr Hoffmann knew a publisher that could help. "Take my advice, and start with a small booklet so you don't risk too much money in publishing."

After his friends left for the evening Sebastian worked long into the night on a manuscript that would become the first part of his *Exercises for the Clavier*. The book was published for the Michaelmas Fair in the fall and was a great success.

Sebastian also helped his friend Silbermann sell his instruments in Leipzig. In Germany they were known as hammerklaviers, but they soon became popular in the rest of the world under the more common name of *piano*.

Soon after his success with the new exercise book, a nobleman student at the university asked Sebastian to write a funeral cantata for Electress Christiane-Eberhardine, the Electress of Saxony. During her thirty-one years of rule she won the love of her people. They gave her the nickname "Saxony's Pillar of Prayer" because of her devotion to Christ.

"I want you to compose a cantata worthy of our beloved Electress," the young man told him.

*Electress Christiane-Eberhardine

Unfortunately, the offer stirred up an old dispute with the University Church. Before Sebastian came to the school, Herr Kuhnau was the music director. He had fought to defend the rights of the St. Thomas School to provide music at the University Church four times each year. The battle continued when Sebastian arrived, and he appealed to the king in Dresden.

The king awarded Sebastian some of the rights, but Leipzig University wanted to limit the performances as much as possible. They assigned the organist at the University

Church to the job of restricting the St. Thomas School to the four Sunday performances. The organist's name was Herr Gorner, and when he learned that he was not commissioned to compose the funeral music, he was offended.

Herr Gorner made so much trouble that the nobleman paid him twelve thalers in compensation. The organist then took steps to prevent any future invasion of the St. Thomas School on the music at the University Church.

During the week before the performance, Herr Gorner sent a clerk to Sebastian's house with a paper for him to sign, affirming he was only allowed to perform with special permission.

He found Sebastian busy with preparations. Copies for all the instruments still needed to be made, and rehearsals were scheduled for every available hour.

Sebastian left a rehearsal with the stringed instruments to greet the clerk and immediately took the paper to show to Anna Magdalena. "How can Herr Gorner be so petty?" he said with a flash of irritation.

Anna Magdalena was holding the baby on her lap as she neatly copied the funeral music for one of the instruments. "Such a furor over a little thing."

She placed the baby in Sebastian's arms. "Here, hold Lieschen for a few moments, and you'll see things clearly."

Sebastian took his daughter and stroked her soft hair as she slept serenely in his arms. He thought of the sermon by

Martin Luther that he had read to the family this week. It was a reminder to be quick to listen and slow to anger. "I'm wrong to be so angry," he said at last. "I must seek peace with the man."

Though Sebastian did not sign the document, he went to speak with Herr Gorner. He listened with sympathy while the younger man poured out how he felt snubbed when the nobleman asked someone else to compose the funeral cantata. Sebastian in his turn thanked him for the opportunity to perform in the University Church.

Herr Gorner was astonished at the gracious words of the man who was called the "princely capellmeister" in the newspapers. With growing admiration for Sebastian, he attended the performance and found the cantata unusually fresh and beautiful. Sebastian's remarkable skills on the organ also impressed him.

Afterwards Herr Gorner was the first to shake Sebastian's hand. "Your choir has been a credit to the university," he declared.

Over time, the two men became friends, and Sebastian supported the appointment of Herr Gorner as organist at St. Thomas Church. It was a friendship that would last throughout their lives.

Though Sebastian won a friend, the university administration was not pleased. They retaliated by persuading the Leipzig Council to stop reimbursing university students who performed with the church choirs when special parts were needed. The council, always looking for ways to save money, agreed to the recommendation.

Despite the lack of funding, the students continued to help Sebastian. With his challenging standards and pure music, he inspired great devotion among them. Many of them came to him for private instruction and went on to become famous musicians and music directors. With numerous opportunities to participate in large productions, they learned skills that would benefit them in their future roles.

Sebastian often wrote recommendations for them. For one student he wrote that he was "diligent and hardworking in such a manner that he not only has helped to adorn our church music with his well-learned accomplishments on the *Flaute traversier* and *Clavecin,* but also has taken special instruction from me in the clavier, thorough bass, and the fundamental rules of composition." As more and more of Sebastian's students made successful careers in music, the courts and cities of Germany eagerly sought to employ his students.

Sebastian continued to correspond with his friend Georg Telemann. When Georg asked for help, Sebastian supplied a puzzle canon for his music magazine *The Faithful Music-Master.* For his part, Georg sent him copies of his works, which Sebastian arranged and performed.

Sebastian wrote his friend with happy news in October of 1728 when his newest daughter, Regina Johanna, was born.

Though Sebastian missed his old friend, he made many new friends among the musicians in Leipzig and encouraged his sons to participate and learn whenever they came to visit. Friedemann had advanced in his musical studies, and Emanuel was making outstanding progress in his study of the organ and composition with his father.

When Sebastian made the acquaintance of Johann Gottlieb Graun and his brother Carl Heinrich Graun, they often came for a meal. Carl was a noted composer of opera, and Johann was a gifted violinist who taught the violin to Friedemann.

"I admire the church music you are composing," Sebastian told Johann one evening.

"They tell me my compositions are too long for Christian patience to endure," quipped Johann.

Sebastian nodded in commiseration. "I forget sometimes that choir boys can stand for only so long. It is a constant struggle to match my church cantatas to human limitations."

"I'm glad opera singers do not have such limitations," said Carl.

"Ah, but you must remember that it is human nature to only sit for so long," his brother said.

"I wonder at that," replied Carl. "Next week I am going to bring one of my violin students. He is a virtuoso, and I think you will find you have the power of sitting as long as you like."

Carl kept his word, and the next week introduced the family to Franz Benda. He amazed the group with his skills on the violin. The bow seemed to skip over the strings as he played even the most rapid sections with unerring skill. The mellow sweetness of the high notes faded on the evening air as his fellow musicians listened in rapt attention.

Carl inspected his watch. "You have sat for two hours, and I have not heard a single complaint."

In November 1728 Sebastian received the sad news of the death of his old friend, Prince Leopold. Over the years, Sebastian and Anna Magdalena had traveled to Cöthen every year to perform for the prince. Now Sebastian was invited for a final performance to direct the funeral music the following March.

With the collaboration of Herr Henrici, he wrote the cantata *Cry, Children, Cry to all the World*. This was a sad year for Sebastian and Anna Magdalena. In addition to losing the prince, they lost their son, Ernestus Andreas, who died at birth as well as three-year-old Christian Gottlieb who died during a terrible influenza that struck Leipzig.

Sebastian poured his sorrow into the music for the prince. He set the verse from Psalm 68:20 into the funeral music: *"We have one God of salvation and one Lord, who rescues us from death."* As he conducted the cantata, these words were like an anchor of hope for his grieving soul.

A comfort during this year was the offer to serve as director of the Collegium Musicum. It was an ensemble started by Georg Telemann twenty-eight years before, when he was a student in Leipzig. The group performed secular music each week at Zimmermann's Coffeehouse.

In the winter they had concerts on Friday evenings, and during the summer they held afternoon events in the garden of the coffeehouse. For the king's birthday Sebastian led forty musicians in an *Evening-Music* along with three hundred students bearing torches in a festive procession.

He continued to work with Herr Henrici and set an entire book of his poetry to music. Herr Henrici was now famous as the poet "Picander." When people praised his poems, he would say, "the defects in my verse are made good by the loveliness of the music of our incomparable Capellmeister Bach."

One bright day in June Sebastian walked through the streets of Leipzig, amazed at the transformation made in just a few short years. He admired the freshly built mansions with ornate facades adorning the central avenues. Some of them were homes to art collectors who opened their displays to the public for one afternoon a week. Just last week Anna Magdalena had taken him to one of these collections, and he came away inspired by paintings by Titian, Raphael and Rubens. The city was becoming known as "Little Paris."

Sebastian turned into a main thoroughfare and entered the shiny door of the elegant Zimmerman's Coffeehouse. Herr Zimmerman greeted him at the entrance. "Herr Henrici is already here, and when you finish your meeting, I want to show you my new clavichord."

Herr Henrici bounded forward from his place at a table. "I'm glad you could meet me—I have a *new* idea."

Sebastian sipped a steaming cup of coffee while his friend unfolded his plan with his characteristic enthusiasm.

"Have you noticed the new craze in coffee?" Herr Henrici asked. "It has given me an inspiration—we must write a cantata about coffee."

Sebastian studied his friend's face to make sure he was serious.

He hurried ahead. "I am working on a humorous poem that will be perfect for the opening of our new series of concerts. It tells the story of a father who will not let his daughter marry until she gives up coffee."

Sebastian contemplated the idea, his eyes twinkling with merriment. "We will need the collaboration of the young people. They certainly know the subject well."

The cantata tickled the fancy of the many coffee-lovers of Leipzig. Sebastian's daughter, Dorothea, liked to tease that the cantata was written for her benefit. "But I will never give up coffee," she declared, as she polished the silver coffee pot until it shone.

Friedemann, now enrolled in Leipzig University, invited all his friends to hear the new cantata. It was a smash hit, and the university students could be heard singing snatches of the *Coffee Cantata* around campus.

*Zimmerman's Coffeehouse

Chapter Sixteen

*Faith looks to Jesus Christ alone,/ Who did for all the world atone;/
He is our mediator.*
~ translation of text from a hymn by Paul Speratus, used by
Johann Sebastian Bach for the cantata: *Now is to us Salvation
Come,* BWV 9

A Pigeonry Life

"I call it our pigeonry life," Emanuel said one afternoon as
he watched the parade of students, professional musicians,
and guests who made their way in and out of their home.
"How do you stand it, Mother?"

"I like the house full of life," she said. "And your father
says there are more opportunities to talk with good people in
a home like this."

In addition to the usual procession of music students,
the Bach home had become a meeting place for the
Collegium Musicum. The ensemble drew members from the
many gifted university students in Leipzig, and Sebastian
enjoyed making the acquaintance of each one. He often
invited them to participate in the worship music in his
churches, where fine musicians were always needed

He challenged them to be musician-scholars—to put

thought into all their music. At the university there there were strong bonds between science, theology and art, and the students were eager to hear about the mathematics behind tuning an organ and the proportion of intervals in music. Sebastian led discussions of the theology of worship and how music could glorify God. Some of his students, like Lorenz Mizler, went on to write theoretical works about music.

One day Sebastian was surrounded by a group of university students. Young Mizler posed a question. "Herr Bach, what is the relation between art and nature?"

Sebastian paused before he answered. "It depends on what you mean by nature," he began. "If you use music as an example, I would say that composers try to imitate human emotions in their art. If you can create music that resembles emotion—that is the highest form of imitating nature in music."

"But isn't art supposed to introduce something new?" asked another student.

"It is a common mistake among composers to make no effort to imitate nature," Sebastian replied. "It is the real art that expresses the truth about God's creation."

Another eager student interrupted. "But you must admit there are limitations. For example, some music is not made for the human voice."

"Ah, but you have it all wrong," Sebastian said. "It is not the music that is made for the human voice, but the human voice that is made for music."

At this time Sebastian received the honorary post of capellmeister to Duke Christian of Saxe-Weissenfels. With his new position as head of the Collegium and the fresh honor bestowed on him by the duke, he wrote an appeal to the city council for better pay for the instrumentalists who served the church.

Weeks passed and the council did not answer. "The City Council is rather odd and not interested in music," he told Anna Magdalena. "They want Leipzig to shine among the musical cities of Europe, but they are not willing to pay for talented musicians."

Despite the lack of funding, musicians eagerly sought to perform with Sebastian, and the church music flourished.

In July 1729 Aunt Friedelena died, and the Bach family grieved for her. For the oldest children, she was the last link to their mother. Sebastian used a funeral cantata that Uncle Johann Christoph had composed. Friedelena had loved this cantata.

Friedemann played the organ, Emanuel played the violin, and their younger brother Bernhard sang with the full boys' choir:

Dear Lord God, wake us up
So that we are prepared when Thy Son comes,
To receive Him with joy
And to serve Thee with a pure heart,
By the same, Thy dear Son,
Jesus Christ, Amen.

Sebastian knew that Aunt Friedelena had served the Lord all her life, and now she was realizing the joy of her Savior.

The next year the people of Leipzig celebrated the Jubilee of the Augsburg Confession. Two hundred years before, the Augsburg Confession was written to explain that salvation was by faith alone. This principle was so important that wars were fought to defend it.

Sebastian performed three cantatas for each of the three days of the Jubilee celebration of 1730. For the first day, he adapted a festive cantata he had composed six years before called *Sing to the Lord a New Song*.

Soon after the Jubilee, Sebastian's old friend from Weimar, Johann Matthias Gesner, came to Leipzig to serve as the new headmaster. Gesner was pleased to meet Anna Magdalena and the children. Sebastian now had four sons and three daughters. Friedemann attended the university, and Emanuel and Bernhard were in the *prima* and *secunda* classes at St. Thomas School. His youngest son, Gottfried Heinrich, was only six, but already showed musical talent.

Sebastian soon realized that his friend was not only a fine teacher, but a gifted leader. He combined firmness with gentleness, and quickly earned the respect of the school boys. He exhorted them to seek the path of godliness and wisdom by reflecting on the day's lessons each night before they went to sleep.

Emanuel especially benefitted from Herr Gesner's

teaching. He worked hard and won admission to Leipzig University after two years of studying under him.

Herr Gesner had great plans to renew the school. He often visited the choir and listened with pleasure to the singing. When Sebastian needed to purchase some motets for the choir, Herr Gesner went to the council and got the money for it. He also began an ambitious plan to renovate the buildings.

For years the school had been falling into disrepair, and the dormitories had become insanitary and crowded. As the snows of January 1731 melted, the renovations began. The entire roof was removed, and two more stories were added to the school. Sebastian's family moved to a house in Leipzig during construction.

While they lived in their temporary home, Christiana Dorothea was born shortly before Easter. Her big brothers and sisters gathered around their mother's bed to welcome the new baby.

Sebastian felt full of thanks the next week as he conducted his *St. Mark Passion* for Good Friday. In addition to his growing family, many university students and professional musicians had become part of his musical family, performing as guest musicians for the Easter festival.

Whenever a musician or other music professional visited Leipzig, the Bachs invited him to dine with them. One evening a choirmaster from Dresden came to visit, and the family spent several pleasant hours playing and singing through one of Sebastian's cantatas. Anna Magdalena and the girls sang the soprano parts while Sebastian and his sons, along with their guest, played the various instruments required.

"I see you have headed the score *Jesus, help me* and finished it with *To God alone the glory*," the man said.

Sebastian rested the viola on his lap. "It is a little habit of mine that helps me remember why I write music."

"It's a good reminder," the choirmaster said. "I hope you will come to Dresden to play your music for God's glory."

Sebastian accepted the invitation and traveled to Dresden to give an organ recital at St. Sophia's Church. The first night of his visit he attended Johann Adolph Hasse's opera *Cleofide*. His wife was the gifted soprano, Faustina Bordoni. She was a small woman with brown hair demurely piled on her head. When she sang, her voice soared to the rafters and her whole presence lit up the stage. Her face was unusually expressive, and she had the trick of swiftly repeating the same note, a skill that Sebastian had never heard.

Sebastian was so impressed with the production, that he introduced himself to Herr Hasse and his wife. Herr Hasse in turn knew of Sebastian's work and invited him to his home. "I own a copy of your *Exercises for the Clavier*. It is well-conceived for teaching the keyboard," he said.

*Faustina Bordoni

The two men found they shared a common love for composing sacred music, and a friendship sprang up which lasted the rest of their lives. Both families visited each other for musical events and followed the progress of their mutual successes.

Herr Hasse and his wife spread the word about Sebastian's organ recital, and the church was filled. A local poet was so enraptured by the performance that he wrote a poem, making a pun on the name of Bach which meant "brook."

> A singing, rippling *brook* to listening ears is pleasing,
> As on through bosky dells or towering rocks it flows.
> But far more pleasant he whose nimble hand
>   unceasing

So graciously his art on all who hear bestows.
'Tis said Orpheus of old, his lute melodious sounding,
Did charm both beast and tree obedient to his will.
How much more wondrous Bach: for sure his powers
    astounding,
Whate'er and when he plays, grown men with wonder
    fill.

Sebastian returned home with dozens of invitations to return. He developed a tradition of visiting nearby cities each autumn to give organ recitals or conduct one of his cantatas.

In April 1732 the family moved back into their home at the school. It contained a new fourth floor with a heated living room and a bedroom. Emanuel, who was now enrolled at Leipzig University, often used this room to study.

The school celebrated the re-opening of the renovated building in June. Sebastian composed a cantata called *Happy Day, Long hoped-for Hours* to be performed at the opening. Herr Winckler, who taught Greek, Latin and physics, wrote the text. He often dropped by Sebastian's room to discuss acoustics and his latest passion: electricity.

Herr Winckler went on to become an expert in the field of electricity and professor of physics at the university. He was elected to membership in the Royal Society of London for his ground-breaking work. In one of his treatises on acoustics, he mentions his friend, Sebastian, as a musician who could "differentiate between innumerable tones."

On June 21, 1732 Johann Christoph Friedrich was born.

The family called him Friedrich. He was Sebastian's sixteenth child. To celebrate his birth, Sebastian wrote a sonata in Anna Magdalena's notebook. He also helped Gottfried, who was eight years old, to copy one of his early compositions. Gottfried was taught at home due to his severe learning difficulties, but the family considered him a musical genius. He copied the tune he composed for a poem entitled *Edifying Thoughts of a Tobacco Smoker*. It compared our lives to a pipe:

> When the pipe is fairly glowing,
> Behold then instantaneously,
> The smoke off into thin air going,
> 'Til naught but ash is left to see.
> Man's fame likewise away will burn
> And unto dust his body turn.

Sebastian liked the comparison between fame and smoke. With his growing family and satisfying work, he was content to leave fame for other musicians. He knew he had chosen the best part.

Chapter Seventeen

*O Lord, how shall I meet Thee,/ How welcome Thee aright?/ Thy
people long to greet Thee,/ My hope, my heart's delight!*
~translation of text used by Johann Sebastian Bach in the
Christmas Oratorio, BWV 248

Zelenka

Among the many guests who visited the Bach home, the
most popular with the children was Jan Dismas Zelenka. He
felt at home with the large family. "I am the oldest of eight
children," he told Anna Magdalena. "Our home—it was
always the bustle like this one."

Sebastian admired Zelenka's work. When he played his
third *Magnificat* for the family, Friedemann asked if he might
copy the *Amen* for use at St. Thomas Church.

The younger children liked to hear about Zelenka's
homeland in Bohemia, where the people spoke Czech. He
told them about the rich Bohemian Forest and the Snow
Mountains which formed the border between Bohemia and
Poland. He had come to Dresden when he was thirty-one,
and he had many adventures. "Once, I played for the king!
We dressed as Arabs, with turbans on our heads," he told
them.

Sebastian's newest *Exercises for the Clavier* became popular, and Herr Zelenka purchased his own copy in Dresden. "Never has there been such a practice book for the clavier," he said, snapping his thumb and forefinger for emphasis. "Now, you must compose the sonatas for clavier *and* violin!" Zelenka was a virtuoso on the violin.

"For you, I will do it," Sebastian said.

When he gave him the sonatas, Herr Zelenka was happy. The parts for the violin were so difficult that only masters of the instrument could play them.

In the autumn of 1732 Anna Magdalena accompanied her husband to Cassel while he examined the newly enlarged organ at St. Martin's Church. The town provided the finest accommodations for them, with a coach to drive them and a servant to look after them. After a week of careful examination, Sebastian gave an organ recital. They paid him handsomely for his evaluation of the organ and for his performance.

Other opportunities to travel came when operas were performed in Dresden. If the opera was by Herr Hasse, Sebastian did his best to attend. "Well, Friedemann, shall we go over to Dresden to hear the pretty little tunes?" he would say. He liked to make a game of finding ways to develop the music he heard with further intricacy. At home Friedemann would play the improvised theme for the family.

Though he enjoyed his travels, Sebastian's favorite place was home. Meals and music with his family were the highlight of his days. In the evenings he often worked on compositions while his sons studied nearby.

One night as the rain pattered against the windows, Sebastian worked in his study, with Bernhard and Emanuel writing at a table nearby. Emanuel was studying for his university courses but clearly hoped for an excuse to take a break.

The overflowing shelves caught his eye and he wandered over to investigate a music score bound in a bright red cover. "Where did you get this?" he asked his father.

"Herr Zelenka brought it for me," Sebastian said. "It's the newest work by Pergolesi."

Emanuel ran his fingers lightly over the rows of compositions. "You must have something here from every country."

Sebastian joined him and lovingly pulled a thick volume from the shelf. "These are the first compositions I copied for myself. See, here are the Bach relations and Buxtehude and the older generation of German composers."

"And this must be your French section—I remember the stories of Marchand," said Emanuel.

Sebastian laughed at the memory of the contest that never took place.

"And these compositions are from Italy," said Emanuel, taking a composition by Vivaldi from the shelf. "May I borrow this?"

"You will learn a lot from Vivaldi," Sebastian said. "That

copy comes from my days at the Red Palace." He thought with fondness of the young prince who had shared his enthusiasm for new music.

Bernhard sighed, and Sebastian turned his attention to his younger son. He had just begun studying music composition, and he seemed frustrated by the difficulty of his lesson. "I will never make the kind of music I want to write," he said, throwing down his pen.

Sebastian sat beside him at the table and took up the score he was writing. "Don't be discouraged. I did not publish my first work until I was forty years old, and even now I continue to improve my compositions."

"Papa, are you sure you are not trying to improve some that are already perfect?" said Emanuel, adding another folder to the growing pile of music he wanted to study.

"I edit any composition that can be improved, even if it is already published. I'm aiming for masterpieces," he replied.

Sebastian returned the paper to Bernhard. "You keep working, and you will be writing masterpieces one day."

Emanuel grinned. "Just remember what Papa says and don't be a Harpsichord Knight—running your fingers up and down the keyboard hoping something will result!"

Bernhard scowled at his big brother. "I know, I know. We use our brains to write music rather than our fingers. I'm just afraid my brain is not strong enough."

His words reminded Sebastian of a passage in the Bible

commentary he was studying. "Bernhard, I want to read you something that has helped me." With his sonorous voice he read aloud: "Thus must the hands work, but along with this labor, the heart should sigh and cry to God the Lord for aid and blessing." He paused to let his son think about the words. "This is why I pray before I compose music. Perhaps this will help you, too."

As the seasons passed, Sebastian continued composing and conducting church music. His older sons were among his most talented students, and with their busy creativity, his home had become a center for all kinds of musical enterprises. The younger children joined in family music, adding a lively note to any gathering.

It was a great shock to the family when later that year, little Regina Johanna died. She was only four years old.

In his grief, Sebastian began work on a *Mass in B minor*. He found great comfort in putting the holy words to music. Once again he found the reminder of God's great love and sacrifice to be an anchor for his soul.

When Sebastian completed the composition, he traveled with Anna Magdalena to Dresden to play the *Mass in B minor* for King August III.

When they descended from the coach, Friedemann was there to welcome them. He had graduated from the university and was the new organist at St. Sophia's Church.

"I want you to see my church before you do anything else," he said.

Sebastian admired the church. "You have good acoustics in this building."

"Come see the organ," Friedemann said.

Sebastian promptly sat at the instrument and began to play. Anna Magdalena linked arms with their son. "We are so happy that you have this fine post."

As Sebastian finished playing, light steps were heard on the stairs to the loft, and Herr Zelenka popped his head around the door. "I am hearing the angelic music, and I think—it must be the great Bach has arrived!" He darted forward and kissed Sebastian on both cheeks. "I help the court orchestra prepare for your performance," he said. "It will be brilliant!"

The *Mass in B minor* was a success. After the concert Sebastian composed a letter of dedication for King August III, while Friedemann and Anna Magdalena feverishly copied the composition to make a manuscript worthy of a sovereign. In the letter, he petitioned the king to grant him the title of court composer.

"This is the right thing," said Zelenka, nodding as he read over Sebastian's shoulder. "You must hear from the king soon."

Sebastian returned home, but a letter from the court did not come. Soon other matters needed attention, and he forgot the petition.

The opening of the summer season of the Collegium Musicum brought a spate of work on a dramatic cantata with the text by Herr Henrici.

"It will be a singing contest between Phoebus and Pan with Midas as the judge," explained the poet. "In their songs they will debate how to tell the difference between high and low styles of music."

"That will give room for humor over the shallowness of popular music," said Emanuel, who was helping his father with copy work.

"There might be humor in the learned style of high art as well," Sebastian said with a grin.

The new cantata gave the music lovers of Leipzig much to talk about all summer. The weekly gatherings drew large crowds to the gardens along the Pleisse River, where the concerts were held.

The next year Emanuel enrolled to study law at the University of Frankfurt. When he visited home, he told about his experience there, where he directed their Collegium Musicum. He was eager to hear about his father's work so that he could take ideas back to his school.

"I hear that the most popular entertainments are the solo harpsichord performances by a certain Herr Bach," he teased his father.

"It is surprising," Sebastian said. "The harpsichord has always been used as part of a group, but I have found that it can be used quite successfully alone or with other harpsichords."

"I would like to play one of those concertos that I have

heard so much about," Emanuel said.

"You may play the duet with me on the harpsichord tonight," replied his father with a twinkle in his eye. "In fact, Herr Zimmerman already has you on the program."

Sebastian encouraged his sons and other students to compose for the harpsichord. Within a single generation it would become the most popular instrument for public concerts throughout Europe.

At this time, Sebastian had many occasions to write music for the royal family. In October 1734, a gala was held to celebrate the first anniversary of the accession to the throne of King August III. Sebastian conducted the music as six hundred students with wax tapers serenaded their majesties from the market square in front of the king's residence in Leipzig. There were trumpets and drums, and four courtiers led the parade. As the choir took up its place, the courtiers presented the text of the music to the king and his family, who remained at the windows throughout the performance.

During the same year Sebastian began work on his *Christmas Oratorio* for the Advent season. For his sacred music Sebastian studied the Bible for hours in preparation.

One evening he worked late into the night. He sat on the floor with his Bible and commentaries spread around him, making notes on various papers.

A soft footstep made him look up, and Anna Magdalena joined him, wrapped in a blanket.

"How can you work in this cold?" she asked.

"I keep warm sorting through all of this, and tonight I have made a discovery. Come and see."

Anna Magdalena sat next to him on the floor, carefully moving aside a cello to make space.

Sebastian thumbed through his favorite Bible commentary. "I have been making notes in the margins. Here we have the account of King David's worship of God, and there is a splendid proof that music was instituted by the Spirit of God."

Anna Magdalena bent her head over the Bible and read the passage he had underlined. Her finger traced another note. "What is this—about the *new song*?"

"This is my discovery tonight. The commentary explains that the *new song* sung to the Lord is the gospel! Music is one of the richest expressions of worship that God gave us to tell of His salvation."

Sebastian paged through the Bible. "I have traced this idea all the way to the Christmas story where the angels sing at Jesus' birth."

Anna Magdalena lifted the pages filled with his composition and hummed as she read them for herself. She turned to him with shining eyes. "This will be a wonderful new song for the Lord," she said.

*Sebastian's favorite commentary: The Calov Bible. He underlined many passages and made notes in the margins. Note Bach's signature in the lower right corner.

The Christmas season had barely ended when Sebastian began preparing his second *Exercises for the Clavier* for publishing. They were ready for sale by the spring. The income from sales provided enough money for Sebastian to accompany Bernhard in June for his audition at St. Mary's Church in Mühlhausen. Bernhard was the third of Sebastian's sons to grow up and leave home.

Anna Magdalena could not attend the audition because she was expecting again and her health was frail. In September Johann Christian Bach was born. Sebastian, who was working on his *Italian Concerto* for the harpsichord, played the music softly as a lullaby for the new baby, who became known as Christel to his family. He was a healthy boy, and the children enjoyed having a baby in the house again.

At this time Sebastian drew up a family genealogy for his children. "These are the descendants of Veit Bach from the sixteenth century, and you will see that for the next 150 years all but seven of his male descendants were musicians. You have more than thirty cousins who are organists, choirmasters and town musicians," he said. "Perhaps our newest Bach will be a musician too."

Chapter Eighteen

...the aim and final reason of all music should be none else but the glory of God and recreation of the mind.
Johann Sebastian Bach in *Precepts and Principles for Playing the Thorough-Bass*

Royal Court Composer

Sebastian walked home through the heavy November snow. Lights from the shops illumined the street, but even with these patches of light, he could not avoid the icy puddles in the road. As he splashed through them, he thought of the melodies he was writing for the *Musical Songbook* for Herr Schemelli. It was an amusing project, giving him the chance to write tunes for several old hymns. There were other hymns that Schemelli wanted him to improve by adding a bass line.

At last he reached the shelter of the school courtyard and opened the oak door of his home. Anna Magdalena met him at once. She held a candle and her face puckered with worry. "I've been expecting you this half hour," she said.

Sebastian hung his dripping coat on a peg. "It was only a late rehearsal for the Collegium Musicum. No cause for worry."

When they entered the drawing room, he found the family gathered around the blazing fire. The younger children were scrubbed and wearing their Sunday suits. The girls had ribbons in their hair. Lieschen ran and hugged her father.

"What is this?" Sebastian asked.

Anna Magdalena led him to his chair, and Dorothea came forward with a sealed envelope in her hand. "This was brought for you today by royal messenger," she said, her voice rising with excitement.

"Open it, Papa," Friedrich and Lieschen exclaimed, bouncing in their places. Dorothea looked at them sternly and they subsided on the couch. The room grew quiet, and only the snap of the broken seal and the rustle of unfolding parchment were heard.

"It is from the royal court," Sebastian announced. There was a pause while he read the document. "I have been appointed Royal Court Composer!"

The children whooped joyfully, and Dorothea brought out an apple cake, still steaming hot from the oven. "Time to celebrate," she said.

In early December of 1736 Sebastian traveled to Dresden to receive his title. At the same time, he was invited to inaugurate the new organ at the Church of Our Lady there. He delighted to see many old friends. Herr Hasse and Faustina, greeted Sebastian warmly. They still lived at court. He was composing operas, and his wife was starring in them.

*Johann Adolph Hasse

The Russian ambassador, Count von Keyserlingk, presented Sebastian with the title at an official ceremony, while Sebastian's friend Jan Zelenka looked on. Other friends were there as well, and they congratulated him on his appointment as Royal Court Composer. They filled the church with a crowd eager to listen to the angelic music of Herr Bach.

Back at home Sebastian threw himself into revising and expanding his *St. Matthew Passion* in preparation for another performance. He created a calligraphied copy that he hoped would be his legacy to the church. In his heart he knew it was his best work.

Meanwhile, Sebastian found fresh challenges at the school. When Herr Gesner left to become the dean of a college, Herr Ernesti became the headmaster. He was a distant relative of Sebastian's first headmaster and had begun as a teacher at the school. Over the years he had been a godfather to two of Sebastian's children.

Sebastian was supportive of his friend, but he soon discovered that Herr Ernesti wanted to change the school. He thought the classics and theology were no longer helpful for modern education, and he did not think music was important. In three short years he had made sweeping changes to the curriculum, which caused Sebastian to shake his head with worry. One day he took his concerns to Herr Ernesti in his office.

"Your cousin would have given more time to training the choir," Sebastian said. "These students are here on scholarship so that they can provide the music for our churches."

"They have enough time to learn simple chorales," Herr Ernesti replied.

Sebastian pulled out a piece of paper to demonstrate the problem. "See here: we need at least eight well-trained singers for each of our four churches, and we don't have even half of what we need."

Herr Ernesti made a dismissive gesture. "Bah, your standards are too high. If we have a solo in each church, we should be content."

Sebastian, shaking his head with concern, left the headmaster's office. How could he explain that the worship service was the most important work in the school, and indeed, in all of life? Though Herr Ernesti was a good friend, Sebastian realized they would never agree on the importance of music in the life of the school.

Herr Ernesti began to resent Sebastian's work and made it clear that he had no respect for music. Whenever he saw students practicing, he chided them and said, "Do you want to become a beer fiddler?" He interfered with the discipline of the choirs and threatened one of Sebastian's prefects with a public caning so that the boy fled Leipzig to avoid harm to his future career. Bach tried to intercede on his behalf, but the young prefect could not risk staying.

Herr Ernesti then appointed a prefect to take his place. The young man had so little musical ability that he could not give the beat at choir practice. Sebastian demoted him and chose his own prefect. He told Herr Ernesti that the responsibility to appoint the prefects resided with the music director. Herr Ernesti refused to discuss the matter and restored his prefect to the position. He told the students not to listen to Herr Bach or the prefect he assigned.

Sebastian appealed to the council, and they required the headmaster to defend his actions. Herr Ernesti wrote letters full of spiteful recriminations, which did nothing to further his defense. He even contradicted Sebastian's judgment that the prefect who led the first choir must understand music.

Nevertheless, the council was reluctant to make a decision in the matter. Sebastian had to direct the first choir himself since Herr Ernesti's prefect could not lead music.

After fourteen months of waiting for help, Sebastian sent an appeal to the king at Dresden. The royal decree came back in favor of Sebastian, and the council directed Herr Ernesti to restore Sebastian's right to choose prefects. They also required him to tell the students to obey their music director.

Sebastian was relieved when the council finally acted. He hoped his work in the community could flourish. He was encouraged when the council asked him to compose a concert of *Evening-Music* for the university students to perform in honor of the marriage of Princess Amalia. The musicians of the Collegium Musicum had a chance to shine, and the concert caused a great stir.

Soon after the festivities Johann Elias Bach came to live with Sebastian's family to serve as a secretary and tutor. He had been a divinity student at Jena with hopes of becoming a choirmaster one day. He needed to work before he finished his degree, and he hoped to learn from his famous cousin. Sebastian made arrangements for him to tutor the younger boys.

Elias was the grandson of Sebastian's uncle, but soon he seemed more like an elder brother to the children. He called Anna Magdalena "our dear aunt" and Sebastian "our dear Herr Papa." He liked to arrange gifts and surprises for the family. When he learned that Anna Magdalena loved her garden, he asked his mother to send her some yellow carnations to plant. She was delighted with the flowers and took great pleasure tending them.

Elias often took the children for walks in the gardens around Leipzig or to hear a singing linnet in one of the shops. His primary students were Gottfried, who was fourteen, and Friedrich, who was six, but he included the younger children too. Lieschen was eleven, and Christel was three. When schoolwork was done, they clamored for Elias to tell them stories.

One day he began a story with his usual mischievous smile. He sat with the new baby, Johanna Carolina, asleep on his lap. "They say that Herr Bach is in the habit of dressing as a village schoolmaster and playing the organ in country churches."

The younger children giggled with pleasure. "Tell us more, Elias!"

Elias lowered his voice to a whisper so as not to wake the baby. "They say that when the country folk hear the marvelous music, they tell each other this must be Herr Bach or... the Devil himself!"

The children shivered in joyful expectation of more stories, but their father heard the last part of the story, and he roared with laughter. "That is an old tale, Elias, and completely false!"

Elias was not abashed. He winked at Friedrich. "What

else would you expect Herr Bach to say?"

At this time Sebastian was worried about his third son, Bernhard. Unlike his two older brothers, he did not attend the university. He went to work as organist at Mühlhausen, but it was soon apparent that he was too young to manage on his own. He got into debt and had to leave town.

Sebastian paid his debts for him and helped him get a post at Sangerhausen as organist. The next year he got into debt and ran away again. Sebastian was heartbroken and wrote to Herr Klemm, who had provided a home for the young man in Sangerhausen:

> What can I do or say more: my warnings having failed, and my loving care and help having proved unavailing? I can only bear my cares in patience and commend my undutiful boy to God's mercy, never doubting that He will hear my sorrow-stricken prayer and in His good time bring my son to understand that the path of conversion leads to Him.

It seemed the young man did reform. The next year he went to Jena to study law. However, in 1739 Sebastian received the sad news that he had died. He was only twenty-four years old. Dorothea took his death especially hard. This was her little brother whom she had cared for when their mother died. "Who knows what music he might have made," she told her father.

Sebastian grieved with her.

Emanuel completed his law degree and was appointed

court musician to the crown prince of Prussia, who would one day be known as Frederick the Great. With his university degree, Emanuel had a brilliant career before him. Higher education made the difference between those who were mere performers and those who held respected positions at court.

In August 1739 Friedemann came home for four weeks, bringing two colleagues with him. They were famous lutenists, and the trio hosted over a dozen musical evenings in the Bach home for friends and family. They also helped with the music for an important inauguration ceremony.

The next day Dorothea ran in to Sebastian's study. "Look, Papa, you are mentioned in the newspaper."

Sebastian rubbed his eyes, which were bothering him more and more. "What does the esteemed newspaper say?"

Dorothea began reading. "For the inauguration of the City Council the Royal and Electoral Court Composer and Capellmeister, Herr Johann Sebastian Bach, performed a music that was as artful as it was pleasant; its text was *We thank you, God, we thank you.*"

"Friedemann will be pleased that our music was noticed, but I am most proud that God was thanked," he said.

Before they left, the lutenists tried to convince Sebastian to travel with them as a concert musician.

"I'm in the place I belong," he said. "I have my family around me and use my gifts for the Lord—my highest goal."

Chapter Nineteen

The Well-Tempered Clavier

In the summer of 1741 Sebastian visited Emanuel in Berlin. Emanuel was eager to hear the news from the family. "Is cousin Elias still living with you?"

"Yes, and he has become indispensible to your mother and me. He has resumed his studies at the university, but he spends a great deal of time preparing Gottfried and Friedrich for church membership."

"Gottfried is no better?"

Sebastian sighed. "I'm afraid he will always need someone to look after him, though he is still as musical as ever." He wandered over to the clavichord and saw copies of his third and fourth volumes of the *Exercises for the Clavier* propped on the music stand.

"Your work is greatly respected here," Emanuel said. "All of the organists want a copy of the third book which they use regularly in the worship service."

Sebastian picked up the slim volume. It seemed strange to see one of his books so far from home. "Elias uses the catechism hymns for the boys. You would be proud to hear young Friedrich playing the *Kyrie* and *Gloria* at our church at home."

*Illustration of first page of the third *Exercises for the Clavier*

Sebastian opened the fourth book. "I wrote this music for my friend Count von Keyserlingk. He has trouble sleeping, and he asked me to compose something for his house musician to play."

"I know his house musician—Johann Gottlieb Goldberg—he was a student with me," said Emanuel.

"Yes, a gifted young man."

"Did the count like your compositions?" Emanuel asked.

"He liked them so much that he presented me with a gold goblet filled with one hundred gold coins!"

Emanuel whistled. "Perhaps you should write some more music for other insomniacs."

Sebastian spent two delightful weeks meeting the other court musicians and performing with them at impromptu recitals. Near the end of his trip he received an urgent letter from Elias. Anna Magdalena was perilously ill, and Elias thought he should return at once. She was expecting a child and could not sleep for more than an hour at a time.

Sebastian hurried home and was relieved to find his wife slowly recovering. She gave birth to a healthy baby girl whom they named Regina Susanna. She was Sebastian's twentieth child, and she became one of his ten children who lived to adulthood.

In 1744 Christel was nine and Sebastian began teaching him the keyboard. Once again he used the exercise book he had begun twenty-two years ago for Friedemann. He had revised it over the years until it was now almost ready to publish. It contained a keyboard piece in every key, and he called it the *Well-tempered Clavier*. When it was published, the book was a great success and became one of the most influential books in the history of classical music.

Revising his work for publication took up a great deal of Sebastian's time. He often added parts to his scores making trios into quartets. In one composition a single staff became a ten-part ensemble. Sometimes he changed a single note to enhance the feeling of a passage. Other times he removed notes to improve the union of melody and harmony. He also corrected musical phrases so the stress fell on the right syllable of a word.

One of Sebastian's brightest apprentices was Johann Altnikol. One day he came with a surprise for his teacher. "My father sent me an early copy of Herr Scheibe's music journal," he said, laying it on the organ in front of Sebastian.

Sebastian frowned. Seven years earlier Herr Scheibe had written a series of articles criticizing Sebastian's music as too difficult to perform.

Johann must have noticed his hesitation. "See here, he writes that your exercises for the clavier are a perfect model of a well-designed concerto."

Sebastian sighed with relief. "It is good to hear this. I had hoped to further the art of playing the keyboard, but Herr Scheibe's criticism made me question if I was doing the right thing."

"Of course you are," said Johann. "Didn't Herr Silbermann write that your compositions are making his hammerklavier the most popular instrument for solo concerts?"

"He is asking for more, and my *Well- Tempered Clavier* is almost ready," Sebastian said. "I am preparing this score for the *E major Fugue*."

Johann eagerly took the page he offered. "Herr Bach, you are the master," he declared as he scrutinized the score.

"But you must admit that you break the rules here in the fourth and fifth bars from the end. This harmony would not be considered orthodox in my school days."

Sebastian laughed heartily. "Sometimes I break the rules if the sound is beautiful. Listen to this." He sat at the clavichord and played the fugue through from the beginning, slowing near the end for Johann to hear how the three parts ran smoothly together.

"It does enrich the harmony," the young man said with wonderment spread across his face.

"If a composer wants to be listened to for posterity," Sebastian continued, "he must avoid being shaped by a distinctive style that will soon disappear. In my early days I let fashion influence me, but I'm revising now."

"I noticed you removed the ornaments," Johann said.

Sebastian waved his hand as though dismissing them. "It was the fashion to overload single notes with ornaments, but I have discovered the essential music can be found without them."

A knock at the door signaled the arrival of Johann Gottlieb Fulda. He was a theology student at the university, who played in the Leipzig orchestra with Sebastian.

"Herr Bach, I have come to say good bye. I am returning home tomorrow."

Sebastian was sad to see the young musician go. "We will miss you at the Collegium Musicum."

"Would you write something in my notebook, so I can

remember you?" asked the young man.

Sebastian thought of a canon puzzle he had played with once, and decided to copy it in the notebook. It had two melodies with the first beginning in a descent to show grief and the second beginning with an ascent to symbolize that grief will turn to happiness one day.

In shape it resembled a crown, so next to the musical score he wrote in Latin: "Symbol, Christ will crown those who carry his cross."

Next to this he wrote a second inscription in Latin: "J. S. Bach wanted to commend himself to the Lord Possessor by means of these notes."

Herr Fulda grinned. "I see a double meaning in that last phrase. Do you commend yourself to me, or to the One who possesses all?"

*Canon puzzle from the notebook of Herr Fulda

Chapter Twenty

*Commit whatever grieves thee/ Into the gracious hands/ Of Him who
never leaves thee,/ Who heaven and earth commands.*
~translated from the text used by Johann Sebastian Bach in
the *St. Matthew Passion*

Frederick the Great

In June of 1747 Johann Adolph Hasse and his wife, the
gifted opera singer Faustina, staged his new opera in
Dresden. It was called *La spartana generosa*, and was
performed to celebrate several royal weddings that had just
taken place. Sebastian and Anna Magdalena welcomed them
to their home soon after their success.

Faustina, in her usual lively way, had stories to tell of the
opera in Naples, Venice, Munich and other places where
they had performed. She also loved to talk about their two
daughters who were progressing well in their voice training.
Herr Hasse had good news to share with his friend. "You
are looking at the new music director of Dresden," he said.

Sebastian told them about his family. Friedemann was
recently appointed organist and music director at Our Lady's
Church in Halle. Emanuel, working for King Frederick of

Prussia, was married and had a child now.

"Sebastian has been invited to the court of King Frederick," added Anna Magdalena.

"It will be a wonderful chance to see that grandchild of yours," Faustina teased.

"Sebastian is reluctant to make the trip until better relations are established between Leipzig and Prussia," Anna Magdalena said.

Faustina's eyes grew wide. "Why, the trouble is past, my dear Sebastian. You must go."

"You will enjoy seeing Emanuel," Anna Magdalena added. "And think of the musical opportunities at court!"

As a result Sebastian found himself packing for the trip. His oldest son Friedemann offered to accompany him, and Anna Magdalena made sure everything was mended and in perfect order. Sebastian polished his ceremonial sword and brought out the silk coat and silver shoe buckles he used to wear at court.

"Emanuel writes that the king awaits your visit with great anticipation," Anna Magdalena said proudly. "You must remember every detail to tell us when you return home."

Before he departed, Sebastian kissed his wife and each of the children. They formed a merry picture on the doorstep of their home as the coach rolled away.

When Sebastian arrived, the king was about to begin one of the court concerts which he loved to accompany on his flute. He stood in the middle of the concert room at the Palace of Potsdam. Huge tapestries covered the walls, and a new Silbermann hammerklavier reflected the light of dozens of candelabra lining the room. The king had his own music desk made of tortoise shell and richly inlaid with silver.

*Frederick the Great playing the flute with his orchestra (Painting by Adolph Menzel)

The band of musicians was waiting for his signal when an attendant brought the king a list of new arrivals.

The king stopped the preparations with an imperious gesture and exclaimed, "Gentlemen, Old Bach has arrived!"

The king was so eager to see Sebastian that he had the travelers ushered into his presence before they had time to change from their traveling cloaks.

The king welcomed Sebastian warmly. "Herr Bach, you do me great honor to visit my court."

Sebastian bowed. "The honor is all my own, your Majesty."

The two gentlemen continued to exchange compliments as the etiquette of the day required. Afterwards Friedemann reenacted the scene for Anna Magdalena and the children, bringing gales of laughter at the picture of their papa and the king bowing and complimenting one another over and over again.

The king could hardly contain his excitement when at last Sebastian sat at the keyboard of his Silbermann hammerklavier. Sebastian played a delightful piece, his fingers flying nimbly over the keys, and the king chuckled with delight.

King Frederick had a large collection of Silbermann hammerklaviers scattered throughout the palace. He now began a royal progress through the sumptuous rooms as he invited "Old Bach" to play on each one of them. Sebastian improvised his sparkling music, and the king stood behind him saying, "There is only one Bach!"

As they began on the fifth instrument, Sebastian paused. "If your majesty would be so kind as to play a few notes on the hammerklavier, I will compose a musical offering," he said.

The king was enchanted with the idea. He promptly sat at the instrument and played a simple melody. Sebastian then began improvising a three-part fugue. The courtiers murmured in amazement, and then fell silent as the music expanded into richer and richer themes.

The king was astonished at his skill. As they approached the sixth instrument he hushed the courtiers who were still exclaiming over the last achievement. "Herr Bach, could you improvise a fugue with six-parts?" he asked eagerly.

Sebastian considered for a moment. "This subject is not suitable, but I will choose a theme and show you how it might be done." He proceeded to develop the new theme with such skill that the musicians and courtiers gave him enthusiastic applause at the end.

Sebastian later developed the composition into his *Musical Offering*. It included a six-part fugue, canons and a sonata for violin and flute, since the king was a flute player. He sent the king a dedication copy, writing a note in Latin: "May the king's happiness grow with the augmenting notes, and with the rising modulation, may the king's fame increase."

On the day after the concert, Sebastian played for the king at the royal chapel and at several organs around the city.

After the excitement of the royal performances, Emanuel took his father to stay with him in nearby Berlin. During the visit, he took him to see the Opera House, which was the pride of the city. When Sebastian entered the large room, he noted the arches in the vaulted ceiling and realized that the proportions were perfect for a whispering gallery.

He motioned for his son to stand with his face to the wall in one corner. Quietly he stepped to the opposite corner and whispered, "This room has excellent acoustics."

Astonished, Emanuel turned toward him. "I can hear your slightest sound—no one has discovered this before."

Sebastian returned home with many exciting stories to tell his family, but of all the stories, their favorite anecdote remained Friedemann's version of the king and their papa greeting one another.

A month after his visit to King Frederick, Sebastian was elected the fourteenth member of Mizler's Musical Society in Leipzig. It was organized for the promotion of musical science and had eminent members such as George Frideric Handel. Lorenz Mizler was one of Sebastian's earliest pupils in Leipzig. He was gratified that his old teacher consented to membership at last. The society required each member to present a portrait and an original composition. For this purpose Sebastian arranged for his portrait to be painted.

Sebastian presented the society with a beautiful canonic variation of *From Heaven Above to Earth I Come*. It was a Christmas hymn first written by Martin Luther for his own children to tell the story of the birth of Christ. In his composition Sebastian gave the feeling of the heavenly angels soaring over the cradle of the Lord Jesus. He created brilliant passages that ran up and down the keyboard to symbolize the angels joyfully ascending and descending.

Anna Magdalena loved this piece of music which filled

her with a solemn thankfulness. As Sebastian played it for her, the words echoed in memories of their children singing this hymn at Christmas time. Sebastian thought of the news of another grandson born to Emanuel and his wife in Berlin. They named him Johann Sebastian Bach. Happiness welled up inside as the family sang:

> Ah! dearest Jesus, Holy Child,
> Make Thee a bed, soft, undefiled,
> Within my heart, that it may be
> A quiet chamber kept for Thee.
>
> Glory to God in highest Heaven,
> Who unto man His Son hath given!
> While angels sing with pious mirth
> A glad New Year to all the earth.

*Johann Sebastian Bach painting

Chapter Twenty-one

...And bring me to rest also./ The grave that is prepared for Thee/ And holds no further pain for me,/ Doth open Heaven to me,/ And close the gates of Hell.
~translation of text used by Johann Sebastian Bach in the *St. John Passion*

Before Thy Throne

Sebastian was working on a new project called *The Art of the Fugue*. His eyesight continued to worsen and he hurried to finish the work. He planned to write eighteen fugues and canons based on a simple theme. He would increase the complexity of each piece to illustrate fugal devices. The final movement was a quadruple fugue with the subject created from the letters of his name: BACH.

"I love fugues because I love order," Sebastian told Emanuel, who was visiting from Berlin. "The order in the world demonstrates the mind of God. It is essential and eternal."

Sebastian was also composing a new *Mass in B Minor*. He used the traditional Latin because he wanted to communicate the eternal quality of God's truth which transcends time and place. Using old and new styles, the composition would preserve a musical art that likewise transcended the ages.

There would be passages based on medieval chants as well as pieces with more modern counterpoint. He wrote a slow section that expressed the suffering in this world, and followed it with the text *"Et expecto resurrectionem"* which translated meant "And I await the resurrection." He contrasted the first sad piece with a joyful passage looking forward to the life of the world to come.

One afternoon Sebastian sat in his office writing a letter to cousin Elias. The mellow winter sunshine came through his single window and made an oblong patch on his desk. In the distance he could see the wheels of the mill slowly turning, while along the river path townspeople hurried on their way to work or home.

Elias was now choirmaster in Schweinfurt, and the two men still wrote to each other. In this letter Sebastian had a surprise for him. He wrote:

> I wish that the distance between Leipzig and Schweinfurt were not so great; otherwise I should take the liberty of humbly inviting my honored cousin to the marriage of my daughter Lieschen, which will take place in the coming month of January 1749, to the new organist in Naumburg, Herr Altnikol.

Elias enjoyed the letter, but worried that "Herr Papa's" handwriting had suddenly grown worse. His aunt had written of her concerns about the eye pains that Sebastian suffered lately.

January came and Sebastian walked with his daughter across the cobbled courtyard to St. Thomas Church for the wedding ceremony. Her new husband had been one of his best students, and he saw Lieschen carrying on the Bach legacy as she became the wife of this gifted musician.

For Good Friday Sebastian performed his *St. John Passion* again. This time he had a larger ensemble, and he was pleased with the work. The next week he met with an organ builder to discuss an organ that a church was hoping to renovate.

Despite his busy schedule, his health was suffering, and his fifth son Friedrich had to act as his secretary. The city council was concerned, and they auditioned another music director for Sebastian's post. However, a few weeks later he was back conducting and performing one of his most ambitious cantatas. It was based on Psalm 72:2 and began with *We give thee thanks, God, and proclaim to the world thy wonders.* He conducted the large orchestra and played the opening organ solo himself.

In the evenings Sebastian and Anna Magdalena continued to play music and sing with their children and other students in their household. One of their favorite hymns was *O Sacred Head Now Wounded* by Bernard of Clairvaux with the melody by the German composer Hans Hassler. Sebastian had arranged it for the chorale in his *Saint Matthew Passion* and the haunting music was still a popular request. The clear soprano voices of Anna Magdalena and Dorothea sang the words while he accompanied them on the clavichord. He remembered both the joys and trials they had shared over the years and was reminded how through all these things, the Lord comforted him and inspired him.

What language shall I borrow to thank Thee, dearest friend,
For this Thy dying sorrow, Thy pity without end?
O make me Thine forever, and should I fainting be,
Lord, let me never, never outlive my love to Thee.

With his usual determination, Sebastian continued to work on the first fifteen of his *Eighteen Choral Preludes for the Organ*, which he wanted to revise.

Friedemann, who was visiting, was dubious about the need for this project. "Why change something that is already good?" he asked.

"There is always room for improvement," replied Sebastian. "And it makes a nice little project for my old age."

Later that year Sebastian conducted another performance of his *Contest between Phoebus and Pan*. His friends in the Collegium Musicum and family members helped to supply the musicians. Sebastian's student Herr Gerlach was the leader of the ensemble now.

During the next year Sebastian had the joy of hearing church cantatas composed by his two oldest sons performed at St. Thomas Church and St. Nicholas Church on feast days.

In January 1750 Friedrich, Sebastian's second youngest son, was appointed to the court at Bückeburg. He was only seventeen years old. On his last day at home, Sebastian chose a chapter from the book of Ecclesiastes for the morning reading and asked Friedrich to read the passage.

"There is nothing better for them than to be joyful and to do good as long as they live," Friedrich read. "Also that everyone should eat and drink and take pleasure in all his toil—this is the gift of God."

"Remember all you have learned here," Sebastian told his son as he gave him a final embrace.

Sebastian missed Friedrich and his help with the copy work. His eyesight was growing rapidly worse and his eyes had became very painful. When he heard that a famous British eye surgeon was visiting Leipzig, he asked for a consultation. The surgeon thought an operation might restore his sight.

"I am still healthy in body and spirit, and I want to be of further service to God and my neighbor," Sebastian told him.

The surgeon was guarded in his promises. "You have overworked in poor light throughout your life," he said. "I will do what I can to bring back your eyesight."

Unfortunately, the operation failed, and Sebastian completely lost his sight. The surgeon performed a second operation a few days later, but Sebastian developed an infection.

In the weeks that followed Sebastian grew weaker and suffered from a stroke. Worried that his end was near, Anna Magdalena sent for Lieschen and Johann Altnikol to come to him.

From his bed he dictated to Johann the choral preludes that he wanted to finish. The words began: "Before thy throne, my God, I stand,/ Myself, my all, are in thy hand." Johann knew that his teacher had little time on earth. As Sebastian dictated the twenty-sixth bar, he suddenly stopped. It was the last note that he composed.

Ten days before his death his sight returned. Sebastian savored a last glimpse of his family gathered around his bed. On the evening of July 28th, 1750 Johann Sebastian Bach passed out of this life and into the eternal hope for which he lived.

Bach is like an astronomer who, with the help of ciphers, finds the most wonderful stars. ~Frederick Chopin

Epilogue

After Sebastian's death his students and sons continued his work by teaching his methods and music to their own students. Sebastian's son Emanuel (who became known as Carl Philipp Emanuel Bach) wrote a treatise called *An Essay on the True Art of Playing Keyboard Instruments* to explain his father's principals. He also collected his four-part chorales for publishing. There were Part I and Part II, and each part contained 100 chorales from his church cantatas. Emanuel was a great musician in his own right. The development of the sonata form is credited to him, and Mozart considered Emanuel the father of musicians like Haydn, Clementi and himself.

Other sons continued their father's legacy. Friedemann was an accomplished composer and used some of his father's cantatas at Halle where he served as organist. Johann Christoph Friedrich was a court musician and composer at Bückeburg. The youngest son was Johann Christian, nicknamed Christel, who became the "English Bach." He was only fifteen when his father died. In his lifetime he became even more famous than his father.

Sebastian's successors at the St. Thomas School continued to perform his church cantatas and maintained the high caliber of music through the years. When Mozart visited Leipzig in 1789 he heard the choir perform *Sing to the Lord a New Song* by Johann Sebastian Bach. He sat up in surprise and declared "Now there is something one can learn from!"

During his life Sebastian wrote five complete sets of church cantatas for the Sundays and festivals of the year. Each cycle contained about sixty sacred cantatas. In 1829 Felix Mendelssohn performed the *St. Matthew Passion* and awakened interest in the work of Bach once again.

The Bach Society was formed in 1850 on the hundredth anniversary of Bach's death to promote his work. The society catalogued and documented hundreds of his compositions. With the popularity of the hammerklavier, which became known by the more common title of *piano,* most of Bach's works were performed on this instrument during the nineteenth century. It was largely due to the groundbreaking work by Bach that the piano came to the forefront as a solo instrument. His novel fingering for the keyboard is still used today.

Musicians of every age have hailed Johann Sebastian Bach as one of the greatest composers of all time. Beethoven called Bach "the progenitor of harmony." He made a pun on the word *Bach*, which is German for brook, writing that "His name ought not to be Bach, but Ocean." Johannes Brahms wrote: "Study Bach: there you will find everything." Claude Debussy wrote: "And if we look at the works of J. S. Bach... on each page we discover things which we thought were born only yesterday, from delightful arabesques to an overflowing of religious feeling greater than anything we have since discovered."

Felix Mendelssohn called his work "the greatest music in the world," and wrote about one of Bach's choruses: "If life had taken hope and faith from me, this single chorus would restore all." The hope and faith that filled the life of Johann Sebastian Bach still lives in the music he wrote to glorify God. His life is a testimony to the hope that is a sure and steadfast anchor of the soul.

Bibliography

Bach, Carl Philipp Emanuel and Agricola, Johann Friedrich, *The World-Famous Organist, Mr. Johann Sebastian Bach, Royal Polish and Electoral Saxon Court Composer and Music Director in Leipzig* (obituary, 1750)

Chiapusso, Jan, *Bach's World*, (Bloomington: Indiana University Press, 1968)

Forkel, Johann Nikolaus, *Johann Sebastian Bach*, tr. C. Sanford Terry. (New York: Harcourt, Brace and Howe, 1920)

Grew, Eva Mary and Sydney, *Bach,* (New York: Pellegrini and Cudaby, 1949)

Leaver, Robin, *J.S. Bach and Scripture: Glosses from the Calov Bible Commentary*, (St. Louis: Concordia Publishing House, 1985)

Marschall, Rick, *Johann Sebastian Bach,* (Nashville: Thomas Nelson, 2011)

Meynell, Esther, *Bach*, (London: Duckworth, 1934)

Mizler, Lorenz Christoph, *Biography of Bach*, (Musikalische Bibliothek periodical, 1754)

Pelikan, Jaroslav, *Bach Among the Theologians*, (Philadelphia: Fortress Press, 1986)

Spitta, Philipp, *Johann Sebastian Bach: His Work and Influence on the Music of Germany, 1685-1750*, tr. Clara Bell and J.A. Fuller-Maitland, 3 vols.(New York: Dover Publications, 1951)

Terry, Charles Sanford, *Bach: A Biography*, (London: Oxford University Press, 1928)

Wolff, Christoph, *Johann Sebastian Bach: The Learned Musician*, (New York: W.W. Norton and Company, 2000)

About the Author

Joyce McPherson is the author of biographies for young people. She has written about the vibrant faith of famous men in a variety of fields. Her lively biographies illustrate the impact of the Christian worldview in Western Civilization. She is also the mother of nine children. In her spare time she enjoys reading history, working with young people, and directing Shakespeare plays.

Other Books by Joyce McPherson

A Piece of the Mountain: *The Story of Blaise Pascal*
The Ocean of Truth: *The Story of Sir Isaac Newton*
The River of Grace: *The Story of John Calvin*
Artist of the Reformation: *The Story of Albrecht Durer*
The Sword of the Spirit: *The Story of William Tyndale*
Beyond the Land of Narnia: *The Story of C.S. Lewis*
The Light of Knowledge: *The Story of James Clerk Maxwell*

Milton Keynes UK
Ingram Content Group UK Ltd.
UKHW021340080724
445336UK00017B/127